UNDER GLASS
A Victorian Obsession

"Victoria, she for whom an age was named."

JOHN WHITENIGHT

4880 Lower Valley Road • Atglen, PA 19310

Published by Schiffer Publishing, Ltd.
4880 Lower Valley Road
Atglen, PA 19310
Phone: (610) 593-1777; Fax: (610) 593-2002
E-mail: Info@schifferbooks.com

For our complete selection of fine books on this and related
subjects, please visit our website at www.schifferbooks.com.
You may also write for a free catalog.

This book may be purchased from the publisher. Please try
your bookstore first.

We are always looking for people to write books on new and
related subjects. If you have an idea for a book, please contact
us at proposals@schifferbooks.com.

Schiffer Publishing's titles are available at special discounts
for bulk purchases for sales promotions or premiums. Special
editions, including personalized covers, corporate imprints,
and excerpts can be created in large quantities for special
needs. For more information, contact the publisher.

In Europe, Schiffer books are distributed by:
Bushwood Books
6 Marksbury Ave.
Kew Gardens
Surrey TW9 4JF England
Phone: 44 (0) 20 8392 8585; Fax: 44 (0) 20 8392 9876
E-mail: info@bushwoodbooks.co.uk
Website: www.bushwoodbooks.co.uk

To Fred, my bolt out of the blue.

CONTENTS

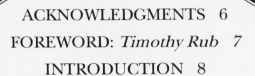

ACKNOWLEDGMENTS

This book has been a dream of mine for four decades. There are so many people who deserve acknowledgment for its realization. Happily, many are still here to be thanked. Sadly, many others remain in spirit only. Living or dead, however, all who have or had a part in this enterprise are represented in some way in its pages.

My memory on this is chronological. My interest in collecting was piqued by my maternal grandmother, Fanny Frank Reis, who gave me a small antique lamp. My mother, Pauline Reis Whitenight, supported my studies in art and my early auction shopping days. My college roommate, Charles Born, patiently accompanied me on endless excursions hunting for decorative objects. Generous-spirited people born in the nineteenth century in my little home town shared endless memories of early times and their way of life in a world of gas lights, beasts of burden, steam locomotives, and sailing ships. An early collecting acquaintance, Carl Wittig, named me "the Rococo Kid" as my interest was so passionate. My favorite college professor, Dr. Thomas Schantz, nurtured my exploration and study of objects. My dear friend, George Gillen, gone from us far too young, must be thanked for his encouragement in my collecting and so must my friends and fellow enthusiasts, Peter and Barbara Avrea. Thanks also to my friend David Harryman who has supported me continuously through this life's journey.

One day, forty years ago, early teaching friends, Bruce and Nella Storm, presented me with a small dome, and from that moment, my fascination with decorative objects under glass has been absolute. Over the years, by myself and later with my devoted life-partner Frederick LaValley, I have been blessed to amass a very large collection of beautiful, even exquisite objects under glass. Travel in England particularly has broadened my interests even more in this art form. My wonderful English friends, Dr. Pat Morris, a noted zoologist, and Dr. Mary Morris, his wife, have provided valuable advice and images most generously. My friend, John Done, has helped me search for wonderful objects, and my friend Anne-Marie Clough, and her fine staff at Focus Packing, have skillfully and patiently packed and shipped some of our most treasured finds. As the specter of this book began to take shape and substance, I benefitted from the enthusiasm of a mentor to many, Shirley Sue Schwab. I am grateful, too, to the many who shared images from their collections, such as Steven and Susan Goodman, David Klutho, Ros Berman, David J. Marshall, Florence Theriault and Stuart Holbrook, Gray Foy and the late Leo Lerman, Joel Kaye, Leslie Orlowski, Richard DeMougin, Sandi Blanda, Michael Sage, Jenine Shereos, Justine Smith, Alan Parenti of Rapunzel's Delight, Martin Langmeier of ide.co Glass Studios in Germany and the very nice folks at Wilderstein Historic Site in Rhinebeck, New York. In connection with the writing, I much appreciate the advice of Thomas Keels and Lawrence Arrigale. I am forever grateful to my photographer, Alan Kolc, for his exquisite artistry and patience in working with such fragile objects, to Romy Burkus for her design ideas and marketing advice, to Sam Gish, Alan's colleague for his efforts, to Linda C. Roach for her skillful editing, and to Christina Harrison, my master of computer graphics editing, compilation and correlation of endless images. I thank Chuck Shuttle and Jude Tuma for the introduction to Schiffer Publishing and to my editor, Nancy Schiffer, for her advice and counsel on helping to make this book happen. It has been a labor of love: I hope it comes across as such.

FOREWORD

It seems as if it were only yesterday that the decorative arts of the mid-nineteenth century in Europe and the United States – a period generally described as Victorian, but in truth encompassing little more than the first half the reign of the monarch for which it is named – were still eclipsed by the long ascendancy of modernism and the taste for simplicity of form and geometric clarity that represented, quite literally, a rejection of all that had come before. Yet it has been, in point of fact, more than fifty years since the first stirrings of a reassessment and renewed appreciation of the artistic achievements of first several decades of the Victorian age began to be felt, first in architecture (what a great age of building it had been) and then in painting, sculpture, and the decorative arts. What the work of the art historians, curators, and, most importantly, collectors who have delved deeply into this field has done is reveal a rich and complex world that seems, at first glance, to be both strange and magical. Upon closer inspection, however, it is perhaps less distant in time and spirit from us than we might have imagined. "Beneath the crass surface," Lewis Mumford observed in his classical study of American art and architecture after the Civil War, *The Brown Decades*, published in 1931, "new life was stirring in departments of American thought and culture that had hitherto been barren, or entirely colonial and derivative; and it is to these growths that we now turn with a feeling of kinship and understanding."

The Victorian home, richly furnished with a fascinating array of objects, was a consummate expression of the prevailing aesthetic taste of the age, one that favored a sumptuous array of materials and decorative elements fashioned into a carefully orchestrated visual ensemble. In addition to expressing the new stylistic trends of the day, which at times seemed to come and go with bewildering speed, domestic decor also reflected the growing prosperity of middle-class households both in Europe and the United States, an admirable drive for self-improvement, and an increasing fascination with the world.

Such is the context for appreciating the delightful, yet little known genre described by John Whitenight in *Under Glass: A Victorian Obsession*, his thoughtful and carefully detailed account of the parlor dome.

An artist and collector who has thoroughly immersed himself in the intricacies of this subject over the past four decades, Whitenight possesses not only a broad knowledge of the field and the experienced eye needed to judge both quality and authenticity, but also a deep sympathy for the wonderful and curious objects which are the subject of this study. As he persuasively demonstrates, contents of the parlor domes of this period and the materials used to fabricate them were enormously varied, ranging from intricate decorative forms woven from human hair and flowers wrought in wool, paper, wax, feathers, or glass, to elegantly choreographed displays of exotic species of birds collected throughout the world.

Part nature, part artifice, these wonderful examples of exacting craftsmanship were intended to delight and amaze the observer, as they still do today. In this sense, they were motivated both by the fascination with describing the natural world (and fixing it in our gaze, much like the new medium of photography did at the time) that scientists as well as amateurs embraced with such fervor during the nineteenth century and the by then venerable tradition of creating works of art of such extraordinary technical skill and imagination to delight the eye and impress with their beauty and intricacy. It is no wonder, then, that parlor domes have the power to excite us as much today as they did the Victorian audiences for whom they were made.

It is difficult for us today to fully appreciate the widespread popularity of parlor domes in the second half of the nineteenth century or to understand the materials and intricate processes required to create them. For this reason, we owe John Whitenight our deepest thanks for the painstaking research he has conducted on this genre. *Under Glass: A Victorian Obsession* contains a wealth of information gleaned from period sources and will enable the attentive reader to understand not only how these wonderful objects were made but also how they, like small cabinets of curiosities, eloquently reflect the art and culture of the Victorian age.

Timothy Rub
The George D. Widener Director & Chief Executive Officer
Philadelphia Museum of Art

INTRODUCTION

The era that was once looked upon with disdain and derision in the early part of the twentieth century became a period of fascination and charm during the latter half of that same century. The Victorian age mirrored the life and attitudes of the monarch for which it was named. Contrasted with the formality and the rather stiff morality of the nineteenth century, there was a spirit of lightheartedness and whimsy to be found in the decorative arts between 1837 and 1901. And within these categories we find the world of the Victorian parlor and its vast array of decorations. The word "minimal" was not a part of Victorian vocabulary. In this world of silk, velvet, marble, and heavily carved rosewood, we find the parlor dome. During the 19th century, these blown glass forms were never referred to as domes, but as shades. If one were to look at virtually any photo taken of a parlor during the mid to late Victorian era somewhere in that room one would find one or more articles under a glass shade. From the standpoint of practicality, yet another distinct quality of the Victorian mentality, what could better protect a Parian statue or a delicate arrangement of wax flowers, shell work, or exotic birds than a glass dome? This practicality was two-fold in that it eliminated the dust, which collected on any and all of the ornate parlor furnishings, and kept curious fingers off of the precious contents.

Romanticizing the effect of the parlor dome, this extraordinarily thin bubble of clear glass creates an invitation for the viewer to come closer and peer into it. It is this rather mystical quality that captured this author's fascination and has not released its hold for forty years. Under this glass dome a world has been created that teases the observer by saying, "Look at me, study me and enjoy me, but you cannot touch."

And thanks to these domes, wonderful examples of parlor art have been preserved from a time when pride in artistry and workmanship was the rule, not the exception.

The technological advances of the nineteenth century were like none before. At last the riches and raw materials from domestic resources as well as foreign were made highly accessible during this "Industrial Age." In the civilized world more wealth and advancement was made available to more people than ever before. Thus, the birth of the middle-class took place. Along with this creation of the bourgeoisie there came about a surfeit of time when people could pursue artistic interests at leisure.

It was at this point that the concept of parlor arts began to develop at a rapid pace.

This development manifested itself in a multitude of ladies magazines or periodicals such as *Godey's Lady's Book* which featured monthly articles on the latest rage in parlor art.

The word "art" has great significance here because, during the course of researching any and all nineteenth century resources regarding parlor pastimes, the author found the word "craft" was never used. One did hair art, or one became a shell or wax artist. One studied the art of skeletonizing leaves or followed a course in the art of taxidermy. And one's hair art, wax art, or shell art was judged by one's peers or at a variety of exhibitions at a local level or at more grand venues such as The Crystal Palace Exhibition of 1851 in London and the Centennial Celebration of 1876 in Philadelphia. The critical standards of aesthetics and art, such as the elements of line, shape, color, and texture, along with the principles of proportion, balance, rhythm, and center of interest, were used and applied to these compositions found under domes. Alas, all of this has gone to the wayside when one considers what is presented to us at our modern day arts and crafts shows held in shopping malls.

Parlor pastimes were not merely relegated to the home. With this fever of decorative art forms under glass, there developed cottage industries in America and abroad that not only sold a plethora of artist's materials for creating these arrangements of wax, shells, and stuffed birds, but also supplied ready-made examples for those who were not necessarily adept. Individuals skilled in the art of wax flower and fruit making, as well as hair work, traveled between Europe and America giving lectures and selling their manuals or treatises for the production of such fanciful arrangements. This was also a time when the art of taxidermy reached its zenith, with hundreds of taxidermists having establishments in London, Paris, and New York. The exploration and colonization of faraway exotic lands, particularly by the British, brought an abundant supply of bird and animal skins, insects, shells, and minerals literally to the doorsteps of these taxidermy artists in London. Family taxidermy businesses thrived and were passed from generation to generation throughout the nineteenth into the early twentieth century. And thanks to explorer-naturalists such as Charles Darwin, the wonderment and desire to acquire things from the natural world continued to become a driving force during the Victorian era. Nature could be neatly "contained" under glass in any respectable parlor, where it served not only as decoration but also as a stimulus for educational conversation.

Along with the taxidermy industry, there existed another that reached the height of its development: the art of creating automatons. In this case, Paris, France, was its center. These delightful mechanical "scènes animée" under domes were created for the sole pleasure of amusement. This is an area where the concept of manufacturing and the assembly line had its beginnings, as these toys for the wealthy were created in a variety of models. As if the mechanization of these automatons were not enough, they also played beautiful melodies, with the pull of a string or wind of a key. As the world entered the twentieth century, electricity would replace the winding mechanism and the grandchildren of the founders of such businesses provided electrified automated figures for store window displays. The parlor mantel no longer reigned supreme as the realm of these marvelous mechanical musical displays under glass.

So, four decades and hundreds of domes later, the hunt and the quest for knowledge about these phenomenal art forms captured under glass continues. This insatiable appetite for things representing another time or world into which we may briefly escape, is the spirit that drives all of us to this glorious addiction we call "collecting."

1

WAX
"BEAUTIES FROM THE BEEHIVE"

Fig. 1.1. Book cover, *The Art of Modelling & Making Wax Flowers & Fruit*, by Charles Pepper and Madame Elise, 1858.

No culture theretofore had embraced beeswax, one of the humblest materials found in nature, as an artistic medium the way the Victorians did. Beeswax has been used in western civilization since the time of ancient Rome in the creation of encaustic paintings and later in religious effigies during the early Christian to Renaissance periods. During the late eighteenth century into the early nineteenth, the popularity of small wax portraits or profiles was common, whether commemorating a royal person or capturing the likeness of the master and his wife from a prominent household. Wax, with its rather plastic qualities, allowed itself to be softened, molded, cut, and manipulated into a wide variety of shapes and forms. Once it was properly bleached to white, colored pigments could be added to give it the desired hue.

One of the many Victorian obsessions was the art of simulating nature in wax, particularly fruits and flowers (Fig. 1-2 to 1-3). The idea of creating arrangements of flowers that never faded or baskets of fruit that never spoiled, both intrigued and delighted. If one wished to have roses mixed with tulips in the same bouquet it was possible. Rare and exotic fruits, such as oranges, bananas, and pineapples, could be combined with the more mundane apple or pear into visually appetizing three-dimensional still lifes that ultimately would grace a heavily carved table or sideboard (Fig. 1.4). These artificial compositions knew no season. They merely existed to please the viewer and stimulate the senses.

Fig. 1.3. Detail of Fig. 1.2.

Fig. 1.2. Wax flower nosegay, c. 1860, purchased in Lambertville, New Jersey.

Fig. 1.4. Wax fruit dome. *From the collection of David J. Marshall, The Antique Room, Brooklyn, New York.*

The Art of Wax Flowers

Amongst the ennobling arts that are taught and which tend to raise the mind above the everyday routine of life, is that of faithfully representing our Mother Nature in her various works. There is nothing more elevating to the human mind than a contemplation and study of the beautiful; and there is but little, if anything, more exquisite in nature than her wealth of blossoms. (Pepper, p. 7)

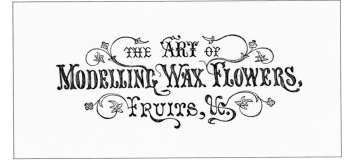

Fig. 1.5. Chapter illustration from Tilton's Wax Flowers, 1864.

Fig. 1.6. Book cover, *Lessons in Flower & Fruit Modelling in Wax,* by J. H. Mintorn, 1844.

The Victorians were passionate about flowers. Not only did they appreciate them as objects of beauty; they even went so far as to give them their own language. During the second half of the nineteenth century many books were published using the symbolism of flowers, the most famous of which was that written by Kate Greenaway in 1885, *The Language of Flowers.* In this small volume, along with illustrations and verses dedicated to flora, we learn that pansies are for thoughts, daisies are for innocence, and the red carnation (pink) stood for pure and ardent love. And with this love of flowers an age of Romanticism thrived and bloomed.

In England, the seeds of wax flower making were being sown in the 1830s. The Mintorn family, who resided at 36 Soho Square in London, made some of the most important contributions to this art form. The two brothers, John and Horatio, along with their sister who came to be known as Mrs. Mogridge, the children of a talented pictorial painter, were presented at an early age with a gold medal for their skill at modeling wax flowers. Sometime later they were appointed as "Wax Modellers to Her Majesty." (Howe, p.149)

In 1844, the Mintorns published their own book on *Modelling Wax Flowers.* (Fig. 1.6). The Mintorns taught the techniques of wax flower making and sold the materials. One of the materials they invented, "The Mintorn Art Fabric," was a wax impregnated cloth that could be readily used for foliage and ground work in natural history displays. This patented fabric gained them a place of prominence, as it revolutionized the presentation of dioramas or habitats exhibited in the ever-growing number of natural history museums in England and abroad. Eventually, in 1880, John Mintorn was invited to redo the displays in the Natural History Museum, South Kensington. Lord Walsingham, a devout lepidopterist, commissioned Horatio Mintorn and his sister to model a number of wax plants for him on which the larvae of certain butterflies in his collection fed. Consequently, the two Mintorns found themselves traveling to America for a three-year commission at the Museum of Natural History in New York City. When their work there was completed they toured the United States and were known as, "The Two Artists who made Bogus Flowers and Plants which Deceive the Eye." (Howe, p. 149)

Fig. 1.7. *Prunus persica,* wax model by Mintorn (19th century). *Photo courtesy of The Board of Trustees Royal Botanic Gardens, Kew, Richmond, Surrey, TW9 3AB.*

Today examples of wax flower and fruit modeling by the Mintorns and Edith Delta Blackman may be seen at the Royal Botanic Gardens Museum at Kew in London. Economic or crop plants, such as this branch of peaches (*Prunus persica*), were rendered in wax by John Mintorn (Fig. 1-7). Mrs. Blackman was commissioned by the director of Kew to create over two dozen specimens of orchids in wax and she did so in a most realistic manner as seen in her *Vanda coerulea* and *Odontoglossum crispum* models (Fig. 1.8 to 1.10). These extremely detailed lifelike botanical specimens remain as a tribute to the Mintorns' and Mrs. Blackman's careers dedicated to working in wax.

Another name associated with the early days of wax flower making is that of a Miss Emma Peachey of London. Soon after the young Victoria ascended to the throne, Emma Peachey called at Buckingham Palace with a bouquet of wax flowers that she wished to have placed in a spot where the Queen might notice them. The Queen did, in fact, notice them with delight and inquired as to who the artist was. Shortly thereafter, Miss Peachey wrote to the Palace informing Her Majesty that she was intent on pursuing a career modeling wax flowers. The Queen suggested to the Lord Chamberland that Miss Peachey might be given a royal warrant and made her "Artiste in Wax Flowers." (Howe, p. 146)

Fig. 1.8. *Vanda coerulea*, wax model copied from Kew's living collections by Edith Delta Blackman, c. 1893. *Photo courtesy of The Board of Trustees Royal Botanic Gardens, Kew, Richmond, Surrey, TW9 3AB.*

Fig. 1.10. *Odontoglossum crispum* (detail), wax model copied from Kew's living collections by Edith Delta Blackman, c. 1893, *Photo courtesy of The Board of Trustees Royal Botanic Gardens, Kew, Richmond, Surrey, TW9 3AB.*

With her royal appointment in hand, Emma Peachey's wax flower-modeler business flourished. In 1840, she was hired to create Victoria and Albert's wedding bouquets in wax, as well as to make thousands of white wax roses to be given as bridal favors. After having such an honor bestowed upon her, orders poured into her studio. Emma's days of having a hard life were finally over. Her reputation gained her the privilege of submitting two entries to the wax flower display at the Crystal Palace Exhibition of 1851 (Fig. 1-11). The entries consisted of two colossal glass domes, each six feet tall, the one containing an enormous vase of wax fruit and the other a mammoth bouquet of flowers that was composed of almost every specimen known to the botanist, *"from the honeysuckle of the cottage garden to the rarest and most exotic from the East."* (Howe, p. 147) Miss Peachey removed her entries simply because she was allotted a booth too close to the glass roof and she feared the worst from the sun's rays. Whatever became of these gargantuan wax arrangements under glass in not known but Miss Peachey, being never one to miss a financial opportunity, exhibited her masterpieces in wax at her home, 33 Rathbone Place, Oxford Street, where it has been recorded she had over 50,000 visitors and the London press who were lyrical in the praise of them. (Howe, p. 147) The closest this author has come to the likes of Emma Peachey's examples is one purchased in

Fig. 1.11. Crystal Palace Exhibition, London, 1851. *Photo courtesy of P. Morris.*

Hudson, New York (Figs. 1.12 to 1.14). This marvelous dome, almost three feet high and over two feet wide, rests on its own custom-made walnut center table and contains a two foot high arrangement of wax flowers in a large wicker basket. It was believed to have sat in the

Fig. 1.12. Wax flower basket in dome on original grooved center table, c. 1875, in situ.

Fig. 1.13.
Detail of Fig.
1.12.

lobby of a Boston hotel for the last quarter of the nineteenth century until it fell out of favor and was relegated to the basement for decades where upon its discovery, the wax flowers were preserved beautifully.

The Crystal Palace's wax flower exhibit did not suffer even with the withdrawal of Miss Peachey's domes, for among the many entries was a full-size specimen of the recently discovered giant water lily from South America, *Victoria regia,* with its five-foot diameter pads and football-sized blooms completely rendered in wax by a certain Mrs. Strickland. Presentations on this scale and quality created such enthusiasm that women now aspired to become true wax artists.

Fig. 1.14. Detail of handle in Fig. 1.12.

This rage for making wax flowers crossed the Atlantic Ocean with great speed in the 1850s and by the time of the Centennial Exhibition of 1876 in Philadelphia, Americans embraced the art and exhibited their talents (Fig. 1.15). One sees in this stereopticon view a display entitled, "Miss E. S[a]hler's exhibit" which included an array of examples without their protective glass domes as well as magnificent examples presented in shadowboxes. A pair of walnut oval shadowboxes similar to the one exhibited by Miss Sahler contain fall foliage executed in wax (Fig. 1.16). The sumac and oak leaves are rendered in all their autumnal glory with hand-painted details of decay and insect damage (Fig. 1.17). Wax foliage examples are rarer than wax flowers and the next oval shadowbox provides an array of Victorian favorites such as begonias, caladiums, and coleus (Fig. 1.18 and 1.19). As seen in Miss Sahler's exhibit, the rustic wax cross was a common and morally appropriate motif. Within the author's collection a similar example exists (Figs. 1.20 and 1.21), but here the composition is all white with intricate passionflowers entwined over

Fig. 1.15. Stereoview image of Mrs. Sahler's wax flower exhibit at the Philadelphia Centennial, c. 1876. *Photo courtesy of the Print and Picture Collection, Free Library of Philadelphia.*

the entire surface of the cross. The passionflower, symbolizing the crucifixion of Jesus Christ, was used throughout the Victorian era. The white wax as well as the choice of the white marble base symbolizes the purity of Christ. The book, *Ladies Fancy Work*, published in 1876 suggests several designs for The Easter Cross (Figs. 1.22 and 1.23).

Fig. 1.17. Detail of Fig. 1.16 showing simulated desiccation of leaves.

Fig. 1.16. Wax fall foliage in walnut shadow box (one of a pair), c. 1870s.

Fig. 1.19. Detail of wax coleus from Fig. 1.18.

Fig. 1.18. Wax foliage plants including caladium, begonias, and coleus in walnut shadow box, c. 1870s.

Fig. 1.20. White wax "Easter Cross" with passionflowers and roses on white marble base, c. 1870s.

Fig. 1.21. Detail of Fig. 1.20.

Fig. 1.22. Easter cross engraving from *Ladies Fancy Work*, 1877.

Fig. 1.23. Passionflower pattern engraving from *Ladies Fancy Work*, 1877.

Fig. 1.24. Book cover, *Wax Flowers and How to Make Them,* by S.W. Tilton, 1864.

The Art of Wax Flower Making

The Mintorns' book in 1844 initiated the publishing of other manuals and numerous articles on the art of making wax flowers which continued through the nineteenth century and into the twentieth. An abundance of periodicals, such as *Godey's Ladys' Book, Peterson's Magazine, The Ladies Floral Cabinet and Home Companion,* and *Art Recreations,* were geared to the needs of the nineteenth century woman who held a certain position in genteel society. So, if one did not reside in a metropolitan area where instructors were available, one had only to subscribe, as evidenced in *Godey's* twelve monthly issues in 1856. The first six issues, January through June, were devoted to the art of wax fruit making and the six remaining issues addressed wax flower making. In fact, this sequence of articles was actually a reprint of a small manual entitled, *The Art of Modelling Waxen Flowers, Fruit, Etc., Etc.* by G.W. Francis, F.L.S., 1854, London (Fig. 1.25). It was, however, the Mintorns' publication ten years prior that gave the list of "essential" materials needed (Figs. 1.26 to 1.28).

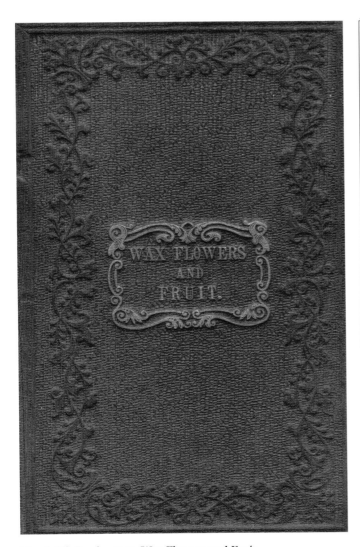

Fig. 1.25. Book cover, *Wax Flowers and Fruit,* by G. W. Francis, 1854.

LIST OF PRICES,

Of Materials, &c., for Modelling Flowers in Wax, Manufactured

By J. H. MINTORN.

	Per Gross	
	s.	*d.*
Wax in sheets, assorted colours .	6	3
Do., medium thickness, do. . .	8	6
Do., extra thick, do.	12	9
Do., very thick and large for Magnolia, &c. &c.	18	0

Colour in Powder, 1s. *per bottle.*

Carmine	Pink Madder
Crimson Lake	Chrome Nos. 1, 2,
Violet-carmine	and 3
Cobalt	Lemon Yellow
French Ultramarine	Burnt Sienna
Prussian Blue	Green
Violet-lake	Flake White
Magenta-lake	Extract Vermilion

Fig. 1.26. List of materials from *Lessons in Flower & Fruit Modelling in Wax* by J.H. Mintorn, 1844.

List of Prices, &c.

Moist Colours in Pans.

	s. d.		s. d.
Violet-carmine	1 6	Sepia	1 0
Carmine	2 0	Flake White	0 8
Crimson Lake	1 0	Indian Yellow	1 0
Burnt Sienna	0 8	Gamboge	0 6

	Each.
Camel Hair Pencils	1d. and 2d.
Sable do.	6d., 9d., 1s., 1s. 6d., and 2s.
Tinting Brushes	4d.
Wires, Nos. 40, 35, 30, and 26	4d.
Do., stronger, 10 and 6	6d.
Modelling Pins, Nos. 1 to 10	2d.
Ivory do., do.	9d. and 1s.
Moulds for Heaths, Lily of the Valley, &c.	2d.
Moulds for Leaves	9d., 1s., and 1s. 6d.
Tin Cutters	4d.
Patterns in Paper	4d.
Palette Knives	1s. and 1s. 6d.
Palettes	from 6d. to 3s.

List of Prices, &c.

Gum Water	6d. per bottle.
Scissors	1s. 6d. per pair.
Wax in pots for Lilies	1s.
Prepared Wax in Cake for Leaves and Fruit	5s. per lb.

Wax Leaves per Dozen.

	s. d.		s. d.
Camellia	3 6	Magnolia	10 0
Geranium	3 6	Lily of the	
Passion Flower	3 6	Valley	3 6
Rhododendron	3 6	Roses	4 6
Fuchsia	2 0	Stephanotus	3 6
Pyrus	2 0	Nemophila	2 0
Orange	2 0	Convolvulus	2 0
Water Lily	10 0	Azalea	2 0

Small Mahogany Material Boxes, fitted complete	21 0
Larger ditto, Stoppered Bottles, a good useful Box	42 0

Far left:
Fig. 1.27. List of materials from *Lessons in Flower & Fruit Modelling in Wax*, by J.H. Mintorn, 1844.

Left:
Fig. 1.28. List of materials from *Lessons in Flower & Fruit Modelling in Wax*, by J.H. Mintorn, 1844.

It was with extreme excitement that this author was able to purchase a full set of wax flower making implements from the 1850s (Figs. 1.29 to 1.33). Not only were the powdered pigments, molding tools, tin petal cutters, and original hand-traced petal patterns included, but also twenty-five gilt brass leaf forms for making plaster molds into which sheets of wax could be pressed. This entire kit is stored in a small wallpaper-

Fig. 1.29. Wax flower making kit, Chester County, Pennsylvania, c.1850s.

covered box from the same decade that is lined in newspaper decrying the horrors of slavery and urging its abolition. On the underside of the small interior box which holds the petal patterns is the inscription:

> *Mrs. Supplee When you use this box use it*
> *Well and do not soil the patterns that*
> *Are in it and so good bye From*
> *Your fine and Most loving sister*
> *Kate Crowell*

(The Supplees were one of the early families of Chester County, Pennsylvania.)

Fig. 1.33. Detail of Fig. 1.29. Wooden modeling tools.

Fig. 1.30. Detail of Fig. 1.29. Tin cutter for wax leaves.

Fig. 1.31. Detail of Fig. 1.29. Bottles of powdered pigments.

Fig. 1.32. Detail of Fig. 1. 29. Brass leaf molds and paper templates for flower petals.

The tools needed for creating such incredible wax flowers (Fig. 1.34) were quite expensive. In the 1850s, one small, gilt brass grape leaf form cost fifty cents, which was the equivalent to half of a day's wages for the common man. During this pre-Civil War era and into the late 1860s the idea of naturalism was prevalent. Each flower was created to resemble the real bloom that served as its model. To accomplish this it was suggested that one have before them two perfect specimens of a flower, such as a rose. One rose was to be taken apart petal by petal, and each one traced, cut out, and numbered in its proper sequence (Fig. 1.35); the other rose was to serve as the model. Roses were considered a good example with which to begin and as one's skill developed one could graduate to the likes of an aster or a large dahlia.

In order to make a wax flower, the wax artist became an amateur botanist as well by learning the anatomy of flowers. Technical terms such as stamen, pistil, anthers, calyx, sepals, and petiole were referred to frequently in the illustrated instructions. Once these terms were understood, the artist could set out to duplicate nature. To begin, an appropriately sized length of silk-wrapped wire was dipped or covered in green wax. A small ball of wax representing the center of the flower would be attached to one end. At this point, if the flower had exposed stamens and pistils, such as a water lily or passionflower, all of this would be created first and then the petals would be attached as they revolved around the internal structure.

Fig. 1.34. Detail of Fig 1.2.

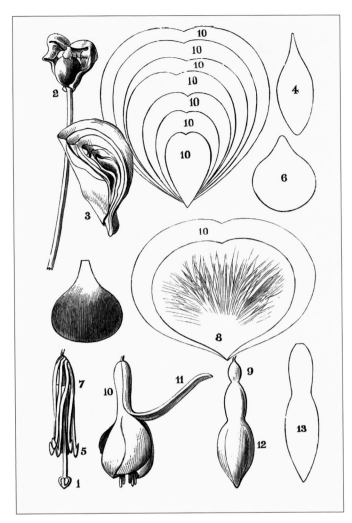

Regarding the petals and the very thin wax used to create them, the artist had two options. The first was to make sheets of wax by melting one pound of white wax in a double boiler, adding one ounce of a softening agent such as Canada balsam or spirits of turpentine (tallow could also be used), plus the color or pigment in powdered form. The mix was stirred thoroughly and poured into a one-inch high square or rectangular tin. Once the wax hardened, it was removed from the tin by placing it in hot water briefly so that it unmolded easily. The artist then would set about making the sheets of wax, which was accomplished by taking a small, very sharp carpenter's plane across the top of the wax block (Fig. 1.36). If the artist was of a less ambitious nature and would not mind having the integrity of the wax flower compromised, he or she could use the second option and purchase pre-made colored sheets of wax (Fig. 1.37). This author feels there would be only one choice—purchase it.

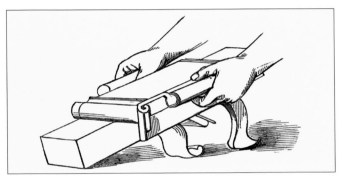

Fig. 1.35. Rose and fuchsia pattern engraving from *Lessons in Flower & Fruit Modelling in Wax* by J. H. Mintorn, 1844.

Fig. 1.36. Illustration of the technique of creating sheets of wax from *The Art of Modelling & Making Wax Flowers* by Charles Pepper.

Fig. 1.37. Sheet wax wrapper, c. 1833.

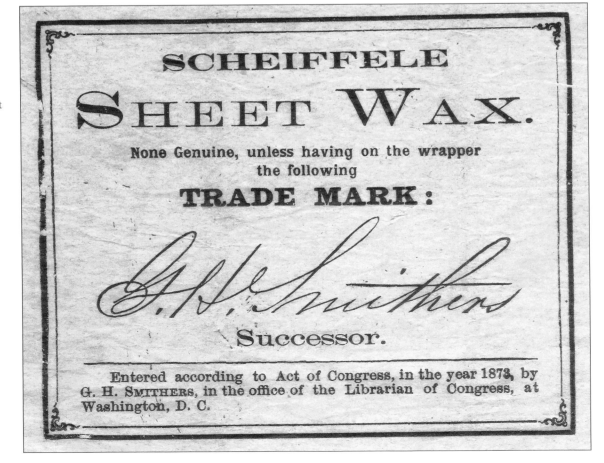

The paper patterns were then laid on the sheet of wax; the petals cut out and attached one by one, being shaped and molded to achieve the desired effect. Painting lines, dots, etc., on the petals at this time could simulate striped, spotted, or variegated flowers. Upon completing the bloom, the artist would attach the wax calyx and sepals under the entire structure and set it aside, moving on to other botanical challenges. After completing all the flowers they were generally presented in two ways. First, one could make a bouquet where all the stem wires were incorporated into a central wire that held the most elaborate specimen at its top, then place it into an appropriate moss-filled receptacle such as a Parian (white unglazed porcelain) or Old Paris vase. Alternatively one could arrange the wax creations in a moss-filled wicker basket with flowers entwined around the handle as well (Figs. 1.38 and 1.39). Once inside its protective dome the wax flower arrangement could be placed in the parlor or drawing room, where it could represent a household of gentility and refinement.

Fig. 1.38. Wax flowers in wicker basket from Berks County, Pennsylvania, c. 1860s.

Fig. 1.39. Detail of Fig. 1.38.

Water lilies were popular subjects for the wax flower artist. They were customarily presented in a low round dome that had a circular piece of mirror inserted in the base to simulate a reflecting pool (Figs. 1.40 and 1.41).

Fig. 1.41. Detail of Fig. 1.40.

Fig. 1.40. Wax water lily on mirrored base low dome, c.1880s.

Fig. 1.42. Chapter illustration from Pepper's *The Art of Making Wax Flowers & Fruit,* 1858.

Wax Fruit

When one thinks of the Victorian Era the words lavish and sumptuous come to mind. What could exemplify these words more than an enormous basket of ripe fruit spilling over its rim? This cornucopia of abundance has been a symbol since ancient times and was well represented in still life paintings, particularly those of the nineteenth century by Severin Roesen (Fig. 1.43). But it was the Victorian wax artists who took these two-dimensional representations and created exuberant compositions in three dimensions. The word appetizing comes to mind, with each piece of fruit at its peak of ripeness, whether it was a luscious apple being pared or the golden yellow of an exotic pineapple. These were the qualities or criteria that challenged the wax fruit artist, all of which, along with detailed instructions, were found frequently in the same books and articles as wax flower making. *Godey's* publishing of six monthly articles in 1856 would inspire ladies to create their own wax fruit still life that would stimulate appetites as well as conversation (Fig. 1.44).

Fig. 1.43. *Still Life with Fruit,* Severin Roesen, oil on canvas, 30.25 x 25 inches, c.1850-1870. *Philadelphia Museum of Art. Gift of Theodore Wiedemann in memory of his wife, Letha M. Wiedemann, 1980.*

Fig. 1.44. Wax fruit in basket from Berks County, Pennsylvania, c.1860.

Fig. 1.45. Wax dessert domes (c. 1860-1880) in situ on a sideboard manufactured by Household Arts of Boston, c. 1880.

These three-dimensional still lifes were not limited to fruit alone. In addition, pastries, cakes, cookies, and candy, along with small glasses filled with beverages such as claret, orange ice, or lemonade, tempted the onlooker (Figs. 1.46 and 1.47). In fact, there are examples of domed desserts where every form of sweet confection is represented in wax. One such example from the author's collection was found as a display item on the counter in an antiquated bakery in northern New Jersey (Fig. 1.48). Vegetables, hard-boiled eggs, and such delicacies as oysters were included in the arrangements such as this example from Berks County, Pennsylvania (Figs. 1.49 to 1.51). Butter molds were utilized, as seen here in the form of a lamb (Fig. 1.52) or in this rare signed wax fruit dome as a geometric design (Fig. 1.53 and 1.54). Although the interest for making wax fruit began in England, it was America that established it as an art form. From this author's experience the highest quality and most beautiful wax fruit arrangements are found predominately in the mid-Atlantic region.

Businesses were created in many major cities throughout the northeastern United States to provide the necessary materials to wax artists, as indicated on the underside of this labeled wax fruit dome from the Philadelphia Museum of Art (Figs. 1.55 and .56).

Fig. 1.47. Detail of Fig. 1.46.

Fig. 1.46. Wax dessert dome on gilt wood base, from the collection of Ros Berman, c. 1865.

Fig. 1.48. Wax dessert dome (c. 1860-1880) with sterling silver teapot in the "Persian" pattern by Whiting & Co. c. 1885.

Fig. 1.49. Wax fruit dome, Pennsylvania, c. 1860s.

Fig. 1.50. Detail of Fig. 1.49. Wax hard-boiled egg.

Fig. 1.51. Detail of Fig. 1.49. Wax oyster.

Fig. 1.52. Detail of Fig. 1.49. Wax butter lamb.

Fig. 1.53. Wax Fruit Dome
with signature, c. 1885.

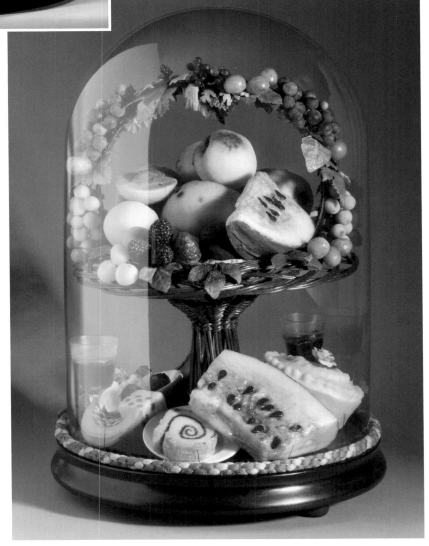

Fig. 1.54. Detail of Fig. 1.53. Wax butter mold.

Fig. 1.55. Wax fruit and dessert
arrangement, artist unknown,
height 19 inches. *Philadelphia
Museum of Art, Gift of John
Whitenight and Frederick
LaValley, 2002.*

Fig. 1.56. Detail of Fig. 1.55. Stenciled label.

The Art of Making Wax Fruit

Once the wax artist purchased the materials needed, including the glass shade and base, from an establishment similar to Mr. Beath's, he or she could begin the process of molding the fruit and other objects. The illustrations from 1854-56 show how to create a simple two-part mold in plaster for an orange (Fig. 1.57). The orange was embedded half way into a pan containing damp sand. A collar of thin sheet metal (preferably tin) was also embedded about an inch from the outer surface of the orange. This collar or wall was to be approximately one inch higher than the orange as well. The plaster of Paris was to be of the finest grade, such as that used in jewelry making, and should have been mixed according to instructions. The plaster was poured over the exposed half of the orange until it was completely covered to the top of the metal. After the plaster set, the tin strip was removed, the mold turned over, and the sand cleaned from its surface. The orange was removed and both the inner edge as well as the outer edges of the mold were carefully trimmed before the plaster hardened. Four half-round holes were carved in the top surface of the mold. These acted later as marks of alignment when casting the melted wax. After cleaning all sand from the orange, it was repositioned exactly as it was and greased, along with the inner the surface of the mold. The tin strip was securely fastened around the finished half and the procedure of casting repeated on the second half.

Instructions were given on how to cast halved and three-quarter pieces of fruit, as well as those requiring three or four-part molds (Fig. 1.58). These were some of the techniques that challenged the wax artist. And then as today, when one sees an arrangement of wax fruit with halved peaches, three-quarters of an apple, or a slice of honeydew melon, it sets it apart from the mundane. After making the mold, the next step was to make a casting. For this the following materials were needed: wax, pan(s) for melting, colors (powdered pigments), a basin of very hot water, as well as one of very cold water, and a spoon. The mold was to be soaked in the hot water (as hot as ones hands could tolerate) for at least ten minutes, during which time the wax was to be melted and colored as for the orange. The two-part mold was then taken from the hot water and one half of it filled with the melted wax, almost to the top. The second half of the mold was placed on top, held tightly and turned upside down and every which way, so that the wax covers the entire interior surface of the mold. This was to be done for ten minutes. Then the mold was plunged into the cold water to set the wax. The wax orange could then be safely unmolded, after which time the artist would trim the seam and correct any defects with a piece of cloth dipped in turpentine.

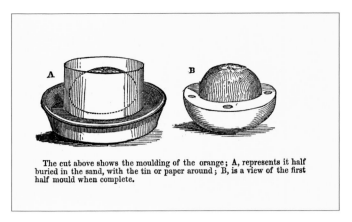

The cut above shows the moulding of the orange; A, represents it half buried in the sand, with the tin or paper around; B, is a view of the first half mould when complete.

Fig. 1.57. Molding of an orange.

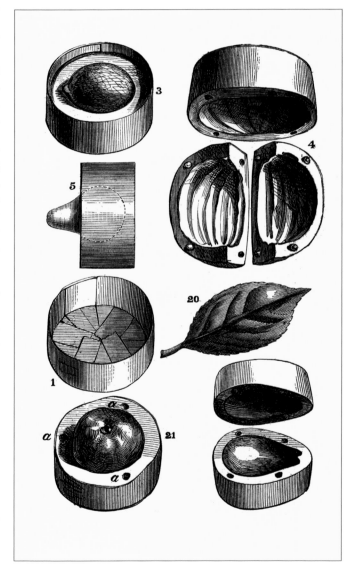

Fig. 1.58. Wax fruit molds engraving (Mintorn book).

The casting process could take as much as one year due to the fact that certain fruits were only available in season, unlike the overwhelming year-round selection we find in today's markets. But while waiting for the bounty of an upcoming season, the wax artist could begin the painting and detailing of already cast fruit. Here is where the term "artist" is not used loosely. Artistic skills were required to create the blush on a pear, the bruises on an apple, the glistening surface of a freshly cut peach, as well as the spots or freckles on a ripe banana. All of this was achieved by mixing powdered pigments with spirits of turpentine or Damar varnish. Cloves were used for the blossom end of several fruits, such as oranges and apples. Real stems and seeds were saved to later be added as a final touch of realism.

Grapes are found in most compositions and they were created by two techniques. Either they were shaped balls of wax with wires inserted or, in most cases, they were created by dipping various sized oval or round-shaped glass balls, imported from Germany, into the colored wax. After wiring them into a pendant bunch, the graduated sizes, along with the thin coating of wax, created a natural translucent appearance, which was desirable (Fig. 1.59). Incredible hues of pale green, red, blue, and purple were used by the wax artist to create these luscious grapes that dangled from the rim of the wicker basket. Smaller, wax-coated, blown glass balls were used to create currents and gooseberries. A bounty of grapes dominates the arrangement of wax fruit in a gilt oval shadow box (Fig. 1.60). Identical presentations of wax fruit done in this manner are somewhat common, thus indicating they were produced at a commercial level.

Fig. 1.59. Detail of Fig. 1.4.

Fig. 1.60. Gilt oval shadowbox with a half basket of wax fruit, c. 1860-1880.

More than Fruit and Flowers

Another area where beeswax was utilized is the creation of figures placed in elaborate settings under domes. One of the finest is that of Queen Elizabeth I bestowing the Order of the Garter on Lord Essex. Every attention to detail is found in this charming vignette: the period-correct costumes, the gilt trimmed settee and stool, and the coupe de velour fabric used to simulate a Baroque carpet (Fig. 1.61). Upon close examination one finds the French quote, *"Honi Soit Qui Mal Y Pense"* (Shame upon him who thinks evil upon it) in minute needlework on the garter itself (Fig. 1.62). This dome was acquired from a wonderful antique shop on Cape Cod and with it comes an interesting provenance. It was purchased by the dealer on a buying trip to Great Britain where it had been deaccessioned from a children's museum that was closing. This dome was one of a series depicting the history of the British monarchy from William the Conqueror to Queen Victoria. As the dealer related, the huge oval dome containing King Henry VIII and his wives was something to behold. With the shipping of such fragile items always being an issue, the dealer purchased Elizabeth and Essex only due to its smaller size and brought it back as a carry-on item, when such things were allowed prior to September 11, 2001. Here again the author asks, "Where did the rest of the series go?"

Fig. 1.62. Detail of Fig. 1.61.

Fig. 1.61. Wax figures of Elizabeth and Essex, c. 1860.

Once again a British theme is used in the following example, which shows us a scene taken from the pages of Charles Dickens (Fig. 1.63). In this case the four wax figures, which have the appearance of having fallen on hard times, are gathered with their eyes cast slightly upward and their mouths agape, suggesting caroling or possibly singing for their supper (Figs. 1.64-1.65). The incredible detail of their clothing—from the hats on the gentlemen down to the worn out shoe of the waif-like girl where her large toe protrudes, all achieved in wax—is a testament to the wax artist. To complete this heart-wrenching picture from *A Christmas Carol,* all that would be needed is a light snow falling.

Fig. 1.63. Wax Dickensian street scene, c. 1850.

Fig. 1.64. Detail of Fig. 1.63.

Fig. 1.65. Detail of Fig. 1.63.

Such scenes that romanticized everyday life of common people evoke the Flemish genre paintings of the seventeenth century by masters such as Vermeer. These subjects had great appeal to the burgeoning bourgeoisie class of the nineteenth century. A *Woodman's Dinner* (Fig. 1.66) from The Strong Museum shows a family of wax figures captured in time, as the woodman takes a break to have his humble meal while seated on a felled tree. Everyone from the household plays a role in this scene,

Fig. 1.66. *A Woodman's Dinner*, wax and mixed media. *Photo courtesy of The Strong, Rochester, New York.*

including the grandmother binding twigs, the children playing, and the family cat looking for a scrap of food. A bucolic scene of a shepherdess tending her flock beneath a tree is a perfect subject for Victorian romanticism under glass (Figs. 1.67 and 1.68).

Fig. 1.68. Detail of Fig. 1.67.

Fig. 1.67. A wax shepherdess with her flock. *From the Steven and Susan Goodman Collection.*

There was also a type of commercially produced small-scale wax figure dome. A large variety of charming scenes were created in wax by either casting or using press molds, after which paint was applied. They are often times referred to as "valentine" domes due to their sentimental themes such as a little girl teaching her dog to beg (Fig. 1.69) or a young lady holding a bouquet of roses (Fig. 1.70). These domes are typically glued into a pressed papier-mâché base and are most likely English or German in origin. A collection of them can be seen on a shelf from the Leo Lerman/ Gray Foy apartment in New York City (Fig. 1.71).

Fig. 1.69. Wax valentine, girl teaching a dog a trick. *Photo courtesy of The Strong, Rochester, New York.*

Fig. 1.70. Wax valentine, girl with bouquet of flowers. *From the Leo Lerman/Gray Foy collection.*

Fig. 1.71. The top shelf of a bookcase in the Leo Lerman/Gray Foy apartment holds a vast collection of wax valentines and other domed objects.

In America, the idea of wax figures and dioramas under domes also gained popularity. Not only the charming scene was depicted; in this very rare and macabre example, one witnesses a horrific subject that depicts an unfortunate scout or settler being scalped by one American Plains Indian, while another has severed the dead man's foot from his leg (Figs. 1.72 and 1.73). The attention to detail in this scenario includes the arrows in the saddlebag and the fringed buckskin leggings of the Indians. Not an image for the squeamish, the knife is poised above the settler's head, ready to remove his scalp with blood everywhere (Fig. 1.74). The drama is also captured in the eyes of the settler's horse as it looks on in horror. This melodramatic depiction of American Indians as savages was prevalent throughout the last quarter of the nineteenth century, and what better way to perpetuate that stereotype than this shocking scene done in wax.

Fig. 1.72. Scene of Native Americans scalping an enemy, c. 1875.

Fig. 1.73. Detail of Fig. 1.72.

Fig. 1.74. Detail of Fig. 1.72.

Wax figures took residence in shadow boxes as well, as seen in this old woman in her ruffled bonnet reading a book while seated in her favorite armchair (Figs. 1.75 and 1.76). One of the grandest and most elaborate examples the author has seen is this entire Garden of Eden created in beeswax (Fig. 1.77). The garden consists of bowers of realistically rendered flowers and fruit of every description. Adam and Eve, discreetly draped in fig leaves, along with the serpent coiled around the Tree of Knowledge take center stage (Fig. 1.78). Other inhabitants include wax birds, deer, dogs, lambs, and insects such as a cicada and grasshoppers. This wax tour de force dates to the 1850-1860 period, as indicated by its faux rosewood case and ribbon molding. It descended from one upstate New York family and made this author stop in his tracks when first seen at The Philadelphia Antiques Show. It was a must have.

Fig. 1.76. Detail of Fig. 1.75.

Fig. 1.75. Wax figure of elderly lady, c. 1880.

Fig. 1.78. Detail of Fig. 1.77.

Fig. 1.77. Garden of Eden in wax, New York, c. 1855.

The Waning of Wax Art

As the nineteenth century came to a close, interest in the art of modeling in beeswax faded. Later examples of wax flowers do not exhibit the time-consuming artistry of the mid-century. Muslin petals dipped or coated in commercial wax replaced those created from micro thin sheets of beeswax. The flowers appeared crude and stylized rather than exquisite mimics of nature. Wax fruit was relegated to being made by using plaster forms with a coating of colored paraffin, which was derived from petroleum-based and fossil fuels. Eventually, as the twentieth century progressed and the age of plastic was born, the world of simulating nature in such a subtle medium as beeswax vanished. One of the last examples of instructions for making wax flowers can be found in a 1922 publication by the Dennison Manufacturing Company, *Sealing Wax Art.* (Fig. 1.79). Dennison was one of the largest American manufacturers of crepe paper and party-related supplies. In their pamphlet they devote four pages to flowers made of sealing wax. What was once a revered art form became pedestrian craft.

Fig. 1.80. Wax flower and shell work arrangement. *From the Leo Lerman/Gray Foy Collection.*

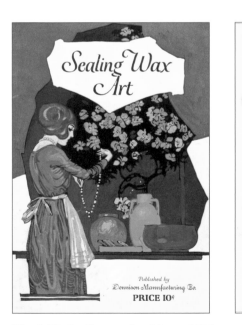

Fig. 1.79. Sealing wax booklet, c. 1922.

2
SHELL WORK
"FLOWERS FROM THE SEA"

Basket of Shell-Flowers

Fig. 2.1. "Basket of Shell-Flowers," engraving from *Ladies Fancy Work*, 1876.

Sea Shell, Sea Shell,
Sing me a song, O Please!
A song of ships and sailor men,
And parrots, and tropical trees,
Of islands lost in the Spanish Main,
Which no man ever may find again,
Of fishes, and corals under the waves,
And seahorses stabled in great green caves,
Sea Shell, Sea Shell,
Sing of the things you know so well.
                    —Amy Lowell (1874-1925)

The mystery and beauty of our natural world is encompassed in one of its largest components, the sea. The sea has mesmerized, tempted, and lured men into its briny realm. Mankind has viewed the sea in many ways. It caused man to question what lay beyond its vast horizon. Along with this curiosity for the infinite, the sea's strength and power humbled mankind so that it became a god to the ancient world. The sea, in all its beauty, offered its harvest to man in the many forms of its inhabitants. That which most represents those elusive qualities of beauty and form is the seashell. From the tiniest mussel to the enormous giant clam of the Pacific Ocean, seashells have provided man with a vast array of shapes, colors and textures which he has used in every way, from being currency to becoming motifs in art and architecture.

In western civilization, the use of the seashell in art continued as a decorative device, but by the time of the Enlightenment Period in Europe it became a focus of the increasing interest in the natural sciences. This fascination with the natural world gave rise to the categorizaton and classification of species thus creating many areas of study. The seashell became the obsession with those known as conchologists. These conchological curiosities created a passion in those who wished to collect them. The rarest, most beautiful or unusual were considered prize possessions.

During the sixteenth, seventeenth, and eighteenth centuries in Europe, the taste for shell work decoration reached its zenith with the building of many grotto-like rooms in the homes and palaces of the aristocracy. Thus was born the age of the "Rocaille," parent to the Rococo period. Rocaille, from the French word meaning rockwork, included the use of rocks and seashells as surface embellishment. During Georgian times in England one enthusiast for shell work (and all parlor arts) was the grand dame of genteel society, Mary Delany (1700-1788). In her memoirs of 1734 she wrote:

I have got a new madness. I am running wild after shells.

Not being satisfied with only collecting shells, her thoughts turned to shells as decorations when she wrote in her diary of 1745:

I have been sorting mosses and ores, and am going to arrange my shells, and to cover two large vases for my garden.

Fig. 2.2. Shell flower arrangement, Latter half of 19th century. *Gift of Mitzi Pereya in memory of Mary Sequin, photo courtesy of Brooklyn Museum.*

Mary's shell work became a favorite of her good friend Margaret Cavendish Bentinck (1714-1785), the Duchess of Portland, who was the largest collector of shells (and everything else) in Europe. Mary created items ranging from small shell-covered frames to designing a shell grotto at Bulstrode Park, the duchess's estate in Buckinghamshire. (We will discuss Mary Delany later in the chapter involving paper flowers). Throughout Europe and Great Britain shell grottoes and shell cottages provided romantic escapes from the daily routine of the wealthy. One marvelous example is the Shell House on the grounds of Goodwood House in Chichester, West Sussex (Figs. 2.3 and 2.4). This delightful garden folly covered with over 500,000 shells and fossils was the project of the second Duchess of Richmond, Sarah Richmond (1705-1751), along with her daughters Caroline and Emily. Begun in 1739, it took eight years to complete using shells from the shores of Great Britain along with those from the West Indies, as evidenced by the report from the captain of the HMS *Diamond* of the same year, who wrote, "I have a small ship load of shells for the Dukes of Bedford and Richmond." It is presumed the duchess had some professional help in creating such a perfect shell interior. During this period skilled craftsmen were available for such work that required the level of precision seen here.

Fig. 2.4. Detail of Fig. 2.3.

Fig. 2.3. Shell House interior, Goodwood House, West Sussex, U.K. *By permission of the trustees of the Goodwood Collection and Clive Boursnell.*

In 1795, two spinster cousins, Jane and Mary Parminter, purchased 15 acres of land near Exmouth, in Devon. It was there that A La Ronde, one of the most unusual homes in Great Britain, was built, having sixteen sides and diamond shaped windows. Supposedly the design was based on the Basilica of San Vitale in Ravenna after the cousins had visited that church on their Grand Tour of Europe. A mid-19th century scale model of the house sits beneath a glass shade in the drawing room (Fig. 2.5). The interior decoration, done by the Parminters using both shell work and feather work, is as unique as the exterior design. Wrapping around a 35 foot high central hallway, called "The Octagon," is a gallery of the cousins' handiwork that consists of shell-covered walls in various patterns, with portraits of birds done in natural feathers (Figs. 2.6 and 2.7). The shells were collected by Jane and Mary from the local seaside as well as from their travels. A chimneypiece in the drawing room displays two shell work studies on the mantle, along with a treasure trove of large exotic shells and corals covering the hearth (Fig. 2.8). In 1811, the year of Jane's death, a chapel called "Point-in-View" (named after the inscription, "Some point in view – we all pursue" on one of the interior walls) was completed, along with a small school for girls and almshouses for four maiden ladies of at least 50 years of age. Mary, who died in 1849, stipulated in her will that the property could only be inherited by "unmarried kinswomen." Until 1886, when a Reverend Reichel, a brother of one of the former occupants, took possession, this condition held firm. Both Jane and Mary are buried beneath the chapel. A La Ronde will be discussed again in the chapter on feather work.

Fig. 2.5. Mid-19th century model of A La Ronde by Lucius Reichel in the drawing room at A La Ronde, Devon. *Photo courtesy of The National Trust, U.K.*

Fig. 2.6. The Shell Gallery at A La Ronde, Devon. *Photo courtesy of The National Trust, U.K.*

Fig. 2.7. Shell-encrusted surround to a window in the Shell Gallery at A La Ronde, Devon. *Photo courtesy of The National Trust, U. K.*

Fig. 2.8. The shell chimneypiece in the Drawing Room at A La Ronde in Devon. *Photo courtesy of The National Trust, U.K.*

Fig. 2.9. Shell mosaic "Sailor's Valentine," c. 1850. *Photo courtesy of © Victoria and Albert Museum, London.*

As these shell flowers began to thrive and bloom in Europe and America so did the cottage industry of selling shells. It started predominately in the Caribbean on the islands of Barbados and the Bahamas. Native people harvested millions of shells of every description from the sea, and shops were created that offered colorful seashell souvenirs done in beautiful mosaic-like geometric patterns (Fig. 2.9). Oftentimes, sentimental messages done in sea shells, such as "Ever Thine," "To My Pet," "Remember Me," or "A Present From Barbados," accompanied the shell work. During the twentieth century these came to be known as "sailor valentines." In some cases, where documented, one may discover such a "valentine" actually done by a sea-faring man, but for the most part they were an island industry. A rare form of sailor valentine is in the collection of the Victoria and Albert museum in London (Fig. 2.10). In this example the shell work consists of three dimensional flowers wired together and mounted on a pale silk background. It is part of the collection from Queen Mary (1867-1953), who was very acquisitive and had a keen interest in the decorative arts. A collection of her domed objects may be found at Frogmore House outside of London.

Fig. 2.10. Shell work "Sailor's Valentine" on silk, c. 1850. *Photo courtesy of © Victoria and Albert Museum, London.*

Whether used in a valentine or not, these treasures from the deep made their way to America and Europe, where shell artists eagerly purchased them. One of the most common forms that displayed the skill of the shell worker is a bouquet of shell flowers under a glass dome. To this author's knowledge, the earliest documented shell work flower arrangement may also be found at the Victoria and Albert Museum (Fig. 2.11). Comprised of over 300 blooms, it exhibits the height of naturalism in shell flower art, with delicate sprays of lilacs emerging from the central bouquet as well as intricate garlands of tiny shell flowers draped around its shell-covered vase. Dated 1779-1781, it was created by Mrs. Beal Bonnell and her niece Miss Harvey Bonnell. It was displayed on the mantelpiece of the Bonnell family home, Pelling Place, Old Windsor, Berkshire. (The glass dome was added mid-nineteenth century). It was reported to have been one of a pair, the second being presented to Queen Adelaide when she breakfasted with the Bonnell family at their home. The whereabouts of that one is not known. A pair of domes similar in size and composition may be found at the Fountain Elms House Museum in Utica, New York, where they reside in niches gracing the Rococo Revival parlor (Fig. 2.12). Fountain Elms was built in 1852, which would give this pair a later circa date. Shell flower domes were created in pairs so that they might take their place of honor on either end of the mantle in many a proud shell artist's home. Another example, purchased from a Dublin, Ireland, estate auction, illustrates the use of

realism in the creation of cultivated floral species in shells (Fig. 2.13). This lovely bouquet (Fig. 2.14), arranged in an elegant Bristol glass vase, abounds with easily recognizable roses, dahlias, ranunculus, fuchsias, sweet peas, and a glorious red passion flower, all of which is housed under its original gilt based dome.

Fig. 2.11. Vase of shell work flowers, 35 inches high including glass dome, Mrs. Beal Bonnell and Miss Harvey Bonnell, c. 1779-81. *Given by Mrs. Mavis Hudson, photo courtesy of © Victoria and Albert Museum.*

Fig. 2.12. Vase of shell work flowers (one of a pair) in the niche of the Rococo Revival parlor at Fountain Elms House Museum, c. 1855. *Photo courtesy of The Munson-Williams-Proctor Arts Institute, Museum of Art, Utica, New York, 60.108.1-2.*

Fig. 2.13. Vase of realistically rendered shell work flowers, c. 1860, from an estate sale in Dublin, Ireland.

Fig. 2.14. Detail of Fig. 2.13.

Along with the vase-style arrangement one sees examples of shell flowers in wicker baskets (Figs. 2.15 to 2.17). This dome was purchased on Portobello Road in London by the author. Generally, this type of shell flower arrangement fills the dome completely with little or no space between the shells and the glass. Upon removing the dome in order to restore some of the flowers that had shifted during shipping, the author discovered a piece of a London newspaper dated December 1868 that was used to stuff the basket. A technique prevalent in these wicker basket arrangements is the application of brightly colored tempera paint to many of the shell petals, showing the Victorians' love of color and their propensity to "gild the lily."

Fig. 2.15. A basket of shell work flowers in dome, c. 1868, displayed on a rosewood and ormolu pedestal by Herter Brothers, New York, c. 1865.

Fig. 2.16. Detail of Fig. 2.15.

Fig. 2.17. Detail of Fig. 2.15 shell work flower dome in situ, with framed hair work and French gilt bronze ram's heads.

The Art of Making Shell Flowers

Just as in wax flower making, a list of materials was required. Such a list was given in the book entitled, *Ladies Fancy Work – Hints and Helps to Home Taste and Recreations*, by Henry T. Williams, (second edition) 1877:

The implements and materials required for this [shell] work are colors in powder, rubbed up well with gum or white of egg, a few varieties of stamens and pistils, such as used for wax flowers, sharp small scissors, knife with two blades, one serrated, or a small Sorrento saw, camel's hair brushes of several sizes, Damar varnish, alcohol, and the shell-cement. The cement for flowers is made by melting gum-tragacanth and a little alum, six parts to one; when dissolved, mix into a thick paste with plaster- of- Paris, adding a little sugar of (white) lead. Roll this into a ball for future use.

Fig. 2.18. Vase of shell work flowers, c. 1800-1840. *Photo courtesy of © Victoria and Albert Museum, London.*

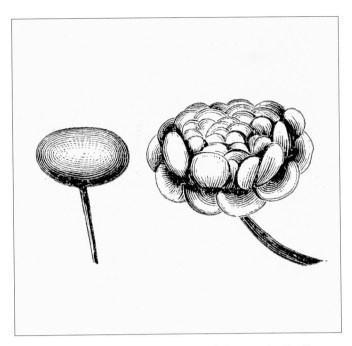

Fig. 2.19. Instructions for making shell flowers, *Ladies Fancy Work*, c. 1876.

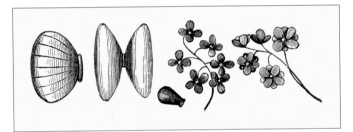

Fig. 2.20. Instructions for making shell flowers, *Ladies Fancy Work*, c. 1876.

Fig. 2.21. Group of shell flower designs, *Ladies Fancy Work*, c. 1876.

A myriad of species of miniature shells were suggested to create the desired flower, such as pearlized turbos, tiny clam shells, cowries, dove shells, rose petal shells, nerites, etc. As mentioned before, these shells were harvested from all corners of the globe, with a majority of them being found in the warm waters of the Caribbean.

To create a camellia, the shell artist would first place a ball of the cement on the end of the wire and begin arranging the suggested colored (painted) shells, smallest to largest from the center to the outermost in a concentric fashion (Fig. 2.19). The book goes on to describe the step-by-step procedures for creating a variety of delightful blooms, from the humble forget-me-not to the exotic passion-flower, where it was suggested one use the spiny tips of the sea urchin to simulate the crown of thorns (Fig. 2.21). Upon finishing a variety of blooms, the artist would begin constructing the arrangement by attaching the topmost wired flowers to a wooden dowel and proceed downward including wired paper leaves in hopes of achieving the desired pleasing effect. This "bouquet" was then glued into a drilled wooden vase that had already received the benefit of being shell-encrusted (Fig. 2.22). Any and all elements of the sea were to be utilized by the shell artist for decorating the base of the dome, including seaweed, coral, small crabs, tiny starfish, and sand. In the examples of shell flowers in a wicker basket, the wired blooms and leaves would be forced into a tissue paper-covered mound of moss that filled its center.

Fig. 2.22. Vase of shell work flowers, c. 1800-1840. *Photo courtesy of © Victoria and Albert Museum, London.*

Rice Shell Work

Along with the colorful baskets and bouquets of shell flowers, there developed an interest in what was called "rice shell work." *Godey's Lady's Book,* published by Sarah Hale in Philadelphia, ran its first article "Instructions for Making Ornaments in Rice-Shell-Work" in 1854. *Godey's* dismissed the brightly colored shell work arrangements by saying,

> *These certainly form showy ornaments for the table or mantle-piece, but are scarcely adapted for ladies work; the plaster stiff wire, rough colors, and actual hard work, being matters of no means fitted for "Delicate and dainty fingers". The shell-work we propose to teach is a very different affair (with) its lightness and purity of look.*

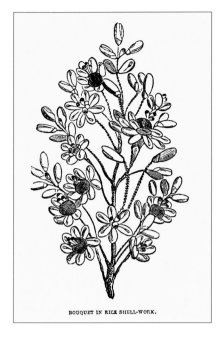

BOUQUET IN RICE SHELL-WORK.

Fig. 2.23. Instructions for making rice shell flowers, c. 1854, *Godey's Lady's Book. Photo courtesy of the Print and Picture Collection, Free Library of Philadelphia.*

The rice-shells (*Zebina browniane*) to be used are indigenous to the West Indies and are named because of their similarity to the size and color of a grain of rice. This parlor art gained such popularity over the next two decades that an exhibit of rice-shell work from the Bahama Islands was a feature attraction at the Centennial Exhibition of 1876 in Philadelphia (Fig. 2.24). *Godey's* devoted three articles to rice-shell work, covering the tedious techniques of the cleaning and sorting to size of these tiny shells. The nerve-racking procedure of nipping the tip of each rice shell with surgical scissors in order for the fine silver wire to pass through was covered in detail as well. The magazine then showed a series of illustrations suggesting basic forms or patterns of wiring the shells (Figs. 2.25 and 2.26).

Fig. 2.24. Stereoview of rice shell work from the Bahamas, Centennial Exhibition of 1876, Philadelphia. *Photo courtesy of the Print and Picture Collection, Free Library of Philadelphia.*

Once a supply of flowers, leaves, etc., was made, *Godey's* suggested a variety of compositions or uses, such as a headdress (Fig. 2.27). For the more ambitious rice-shell artist, in their final article of 1854, *Godey's* suggested a fully three-dimensional basket that could be filled with more shell work flowers or anything else (Fig. 2.28).

The author obtained a magnificent example of rice-shell work under a dome (Figs. 2.29 to 2.31) when it was deaccessioned from the Farnsworth Museum in Maine. Here we see a large rice-shell basket, which is brimming with pale pink and salmon shell flowers, including cut mother-of-pearl as petals and accents. Upon examining the contents of the basket, the author discovered rice-shell earrings and a pin, suggesting this may have accompanied a bride down the aisle.

The ladies magazine also implies the creativity expressed by the rice-shell artist is limited only by his or her own imagination. The art form was not for hair ornaments and baskets alone, but could be used to demonstrate the religious convictions of the household by creating a cross in all its lacy beauty and purity (Fig. 2.32).

Fig. 2.25. Designs for rice shell flowers, c. 1854, *Godey's Lady's Book. Photo courtesy of the Print and Picture Collection, Free Library of Philadelphia.*

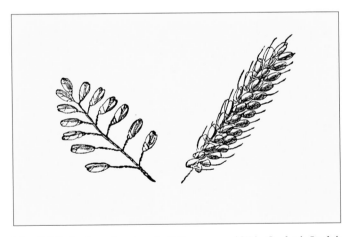

Fig. 2.26. Designs for rice shell flowers, c. 1854, *Godey's Lady's Book. Photo courtesy of the Print and Picture Collection, Free Library of Philadelphia.*

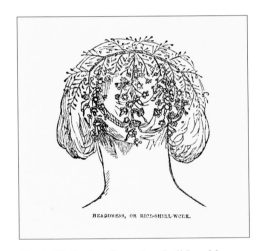

HEADDRESS, OR RICE-SHELL-WORK.

Fig. 2.27. Design for a rice shell headdress, c. 1854, *Godey's Lady's Book. Photo courtesy of the Print and Picture Collection, Free Library of Philadelphia.*

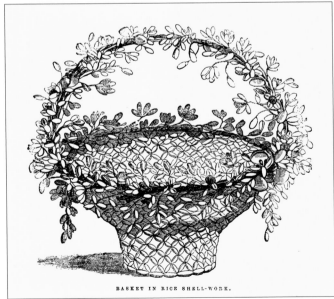

BASKET IN RICE SHELL-WORK.

Fig. 2.28. Design for a basket of rice shell flowers, c. 1854, *Godey's Lady's Book. Photo courtesy of the Print and Picture Collection, Free Library of Philadelphia.*

Fig. 2.29. Rice shell work basket with rice shell flowers in dome, c. 1855.

Fig. 2.30. Detail of Fig. 2.29.

Fig. 2.31. Detail of Fig. 2.29.

Fig. 2.32. Rice shell work cross in dome, c. 1855.

Other Shell Art Forms

As one studies and develops a connoisseurship of these parlor arts, one will seek out the unusual or rare, such as the following examples.

Sold by Christie's of London from the Michael Lipitch II collection, we see an elegant pair of cornucopias turned upward with bouquets of shell flowers erupting from their open ends (Fig. 2.33). Here the skill of the shell artist has reached a level of quality that is beyond the commonplace, with the cornucopias being composed of rice shells on wire along with the abundance of plaster-worked shell flowers at the top. With their glass domes (not pictured), the pair stands 24 inches (61 cm) high. Unfortunately, the author missed these two but hope springs eternal.

Under another pair of English (the English were the masters of shell art) domes, ch we find a garden scene, complete with a fence, tiny plants, and a shell work boy and girl seated under their own spreading tree of beautiful shell flowers (Fig. 2.34). The trees bending in an asymmetrical fashion have a passionflower vine growing up their trunks. The boy and girl, except for their hands and faces, are shell-covered also (Figs. 2.35 and 2.36). Studies of shell work figures were popular during the first half of the nineteenth century. This one of a pair resides in the collection at Winterthur Museum in America (Fig. 2.37).

Fig. 2.33. Pair of mid-Victorian shell work flower displays, each depicting a flower-strewn shell work cornucopia, from the Michael Lipitch II Collection Sale (shown without glass domes). *Photo courtesy of Christie's, London.*

Fig. 2.34. Pair of shell work domes depicting a garden scene with shell figures under shell flower trees, c.1840.

Fig. 2.35. Detail of Fig. 2.34.

Fig. 2.36. Detail of Fig. 2.34.

Included in the more unusual forms of shell art under glass, a shell work bird of prey, perhaps a falcon, is found in a stealth-like pose over an unsuspecting taxidermied mouse as another bird friend done in pink shells stands by oblivious to the scene (Fig. 2.38).

Birds are less frequently represented in shell work compositions under glass. But in this example (Fig. 2.39) one finds a pair of shell-encrusted birds (Fig. 2.40) perched in a wire and plaster covered tree decorated with dry grasses. From their lofty perches, they look down upon a hillside entirely made of seashells. This piece evokes a more homemade or folk art approach.

Fig. 2.37. Shell work doll (figure) in dome. *Photo courtesy of Winterthur Museum.*

Fig. 2.38. Shell work falcon with taxidermy mouse in dome, c. 1875.

Fig. 2.40. Detail of Fig. 2.39.

Fig. 2.39. Shell work scene depicting two shell birds in shell flower tree, c. 1865.

One of the finest presentations illustrating the concept of shell work as folk art can be found in this arrangement housed under a magnificent square-based dome (Fig. 2.41). The theme is a monumental arch (Fig. 2.42) covered in moss and beautiful blooms done in shells that have been imbedded in mounds of beeswax, yet another technique. These flowers are accented with fern-like sprays of rice shells. The columns supporting the arch are not only embellished with spiraling shells and crab eye seeds (*abrus precatorius*), but also have three-dimensional birds feathered with minute rose petal shells and tails composed of tusk shells. Nestled under the arch is a shell work vase holding a bouquet of smaller shell flowers and another shell bird (Fig. 2.43). The stepped moss-covered dais is trimmed with shells and decorated with shell work cartouches. One also finds turtles made of shells lurking amidst the moss. This piece, as well as the one illustrated prior to it, in the author's opinion, has the appearance of being made in America.

Fig. 2.42. Detail of Fig. 2.41.

Fig. 2.41. Shell work arch with shell birds and vase in square-based dome, c. 1860.

Fig. 2.43. Detail of Fig. 2.41.

Fig. 2.44. Pownoll Shell Temple on George III mahogany tripod stand by Mayhew and Ince, London, c. 1762. *Photo courtesy of Christie's, London.*

Architectural examples of shell work are few and far between. One of the most exquisite objects created in shell work is the Pownoll Shell Temple centerpiece, circa 1762 (shown here without its protective glass case) (Fig. 2.44). Captain Pownall's temple, with its mahogany stand, is a tour de force of the decorative arts and was likely created under the guidance of Sir Robert Taylor (1714-1788), who was the architect for the captain's villa, Sharpham House in Devon. The temple is thought to have been commissioned to celebrate the marriage of Captain Philemon Pownoll (1734-1780) to Jane (d. 1778), daughter of Lewis Arnold Majendie of Exeter. Evoking the romantic concepts of eternal love and perpetual spring, this medley of delicately colored shells and golden yellow mica pays tribute to Venus, the goddess of love. Garlands of shell flowers cling to the glittering Tuscan columns that support a shell-encrusted entablature that is surmounted by a dome covered in pink rose petal sea shells. The George III tripod mahogany stand that holds the temple is attributed to the cabinetmakers Mayhew and Ince of Golden Square (Soho) in London. The stand is a masterpiece of mid-eighteenth century furniture design influenced by Thomas Chippendale.

At a more humble level, this petite domed and columned temple of love under glass is from the Strong Museum in Rochester, New York (Fig. 2.45). A small Parian statue of a child stands demurely under a shell covered roof with a finial suggesting a bird on its nest. An unusual shell work can be found in the Robert J. Milligan Parlor exhibit at The Brooklyn Museum of Art (Fig. 2.46). In this dome, a beautiful shell covered shrine has been created. The Gothic-inspired niche, with its shell spires, holds a daguerreotype of a young man, which is tied in place with a silk bow, possibly as a memorial (Fig. 2.47). If so, this is the only one known by the author.

Fig. 2.45. Shell work temple with cupid and dove, c. 1875. *Photo courtesy of The Strong, Rochester, New York.*

Fig. 2.46. Shell work shrine in the Gothic Revival style from the Robert J. Milligan Parlor, c. 1855. *Photo courtesy of The Brooklyn Museum, New York.*

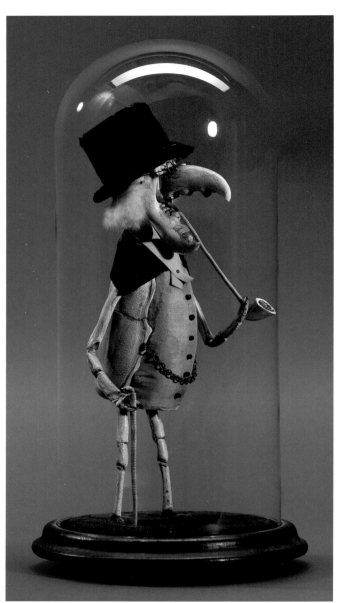

Fig. 2.48. Gentleman created from lobster parts, c. 1867.

Fig. 2.49.
Detail of Fig.
2.48.

Fig. 2.50. Suggestion
for making figures
from lobster parts, c.
1867, *Godey's Lady's
Book. Photo courtesy
of the Print and
Picture Collection,
Free Library of
Philadelphia.*

Fig. 2.51. Suggestion
for making figures
from lobster parts, c.
1867, *Godey's Lady's
Book. Photo courtesy
of the Print and
Picture Collection,
Free Library of
Philadelphia.*

More Than Sea Shells

Using items from the sea was not limited to shells. Other denizens of the deep, such as lobsters or crabs, were utilized such as this "lobster" gentleman under his own glass shade (Fig. 2.48). In this example, one can apply the age-old adage of "waste not, want not." If one were fortunate enough to have lobster on the menu, the creature's entire body was to be put to further purpose and not simply discarded. Here the claw becomes the face, the upper body becomes the jacket, the segmented legs are his limbs, and the antennae his pipe and cane. All the details are executed with skill, from his black velvet hat to his vest with a watch chain, and his pince-nez glasses (Fig. 2.49). This creative use of our crustacean friend was first illustrated

in *Godey's Lady's Book* in 1867 (Fig. 2.50 and 2.51). *Godey's* suggested one use the entire lobster carcass to create a whimsical couple of toothpick or match safes. The reader is instructed to create rather bizarre, bird-like feet out of wire wrapped in orange wool, and to dress the couple as fancifully as possible, using their best sewing skills.

These "lobster people" are some of the rarest examples of Victorian shell work. Only four other examples are known to this author, the first being "The Squire and the Parson after Dinner, 1884" by Mr. Williams (Fig. 2.52), which sold in the Potter's Museum of Curiosities Sale held by Bonham's auction in 2003. In this glass-cased setting, the two gentlemen are seen enjoying each other's company along with their pipes and tankards of ale. Three domed examples are in the Strong Museum, which has an extensive collection of items under glass shades. A game of cribbage is the subject of four lobster men seated at a miniature table that rests on a velvet covered base (Fig. 2.53). Two more round domes contain lobster men musicians, one playing the violin with his pipe and beverage close by (Figs. 2.54 and 2.55), while the other is strumming his banjo (Figs. 2.56 and 2.57).

Fig. 2.52. "The Squire and The Parson after Dinner," lobster parts and mixed media, c. 1870. *Photo courtesy of Bonham's, London.*

Fig. 2.53. Four (lobster) gentlemen playing cribbage in dome, c. 1870. *Photo courtesy of The Strong, Rochester, New York.*

Fig. 2.54. (Lobster) gentleman playing the violin, c. 1870. *Photo courtesy of The Strong, Rochester, New York.*

Fig. 2.56. (Lobster) gentleman playing the banjo, c. 1870. *Photo courtesy of The Strong, Rochester, New York.*

Fig. 2.55. Detail of Fig. 2.54.

Fig. 2.57. Detail of Fig. 2.56.

Shell work also found its place on the walls of Victorian parlors. One archetypical form was the half basket filled with shell flowers that was presented in deep shadow boxes of various shapes. One sees this form in a gilt round frame (Fig. 2.58), where a small store-bought straw basket cut in half holds a charming arrangement of shell flowers with dried mosses and seaweed. On a larger scale, the next shell work bouquet is housed in a shell-covered oval shell work frame approximately two and one half feet wide (Fig. 2.59). Naturalism prevails in this piece that was said to have been deaccessioned from the Henry Ford Museum in Michigan and is now in the Steven and Susan Goodman collection. The shell flowers are arranged in a huge abalone shell (Fig. 2.60). The rustic quality of this shell work may suggest that is was made in America.

Fig. 2.58. Shell work flowers in half wicker basket in gilt round shadow box, c. 1860.

Fig. 2.59. Bouquet of shell flowers in shell-covered oval frame, c. 1865. *From the Steven and Susan Goodman Collection.*

Fig. 2.60. Detail of Fig. 2.59.

Fig. 2.61. Large shell work bouquet of flowers in gilt-over-gesso Rococo frame, c. 1865, in situ with Parian vases and laminated rosewood sofa by John Henry Belter, c. 1855.

Fig. 2.62.
Detail of Fig. 2.61.

Fig. 2.63.
Detail of Fig. 2.61.

In contrast, the following elegant shell work bouquet has a very interesting story. The provenance is that it once graced the walls of Chapultepec Palace in current day Mexico City, which was the home of Emperor Maximilian and Empress Carlota (Fig. 2.61). It was said to have been brought there by Carlota from France. The author first saw this piece in the home of the antique dealers Stingray Hornsby. The purpose of the visit was to pick up a purchased item. At first sight the author was awe-struck and inquired if it was for sale. It was not. There began what we will refer to as "operation pester." For four years at every opportunity the author would ask the dealers if they would sell the shell work. They finally relented. The huge gilt oval frame, over three-and-a-half feet high by three-and-a-half feet wide, containing exquisite shell work flowers presented in a latticed beadwork basket trimmed in faux black pearls (Figs. 2.62 and 2.63) would be worthy of any palace.

Out with the Tide

The days of shell-decorated rooms and conchological fantasies under glass domes are long gone, yet sea shells continue to attract attention with their myriad of forms and colors. Shell collecting is still a popular pastime when one is on holiday, and shops in seaside resorts offer shells from all over the world. Whether building a collection or purchasing them as souvenirs, sea shells remain a popular item. The art of shell work is now predominantly limited to shell-encrusted frames, ashtrays, figures, and boxes that could be described as kitsch. In some upscale shops and galleries, modern day sailor valentines may be found by such shell artists as Sandi Blanda (see chapter 12). Just as the tide ebbs and flows perhaps someday the art of shell work will return to reclaim its glorious past.

3
HAIR WORK
"HAIR TODAY, HAIR TOMORROW"

Fig. 3.1. Photograph of Hannah, c. 1880.
Photo courtesy of Rapunzel's Delight.

When on these lines you gently look
Think from whose head this lock was took
This lock of hair this morn was mine
But soon I trust it will be thine
May ever on thy youthful brow
The wreath of friendship bud and blow
And on that wreath may there be
One blossom cherished long for me
         Helen M. Houghton
         Boston Jan 18 1846 (Fig. 3.2)

Webster's New Collegiate Dictionary, 1977 Ed., defines the word memory as: "1a: The power or process of reproducing or recalling esp. through associative mechanisms." This clinical definition could never be aligned with the sentimental views expressed by the Victorians, who were concerned with the heart-felt emotions associated with words such as memory, remembrance, and memorial. No other parlor art expresses the 19th century's love of sentimentality more than hair work. (Fig. 3.3)

Fig. 3.2. Poem with lock of hair from "Hair Book," c. 1840s.

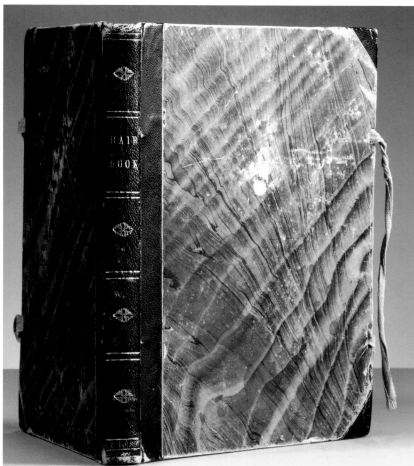

Fig. 3.3. "Hair Book" containing locks of woven hair with accompanying poems, c. 1840s.

Hair is a word that is both singular and plural. It possesses a power that has transcended the ages. It will be with our species till we cease to exist. It may be used as a form of personal expression and adornment or to define one's place in the society in which one lives. Hairstyles have evolved along with mankind. In the nineteenth century, long hair was a sign of femininity and was highly admired and desired (Fig. 3.1). One of P. T. Barnum's popular attractions of the 1880s was the Sutherland Sisters (Fig. 3.4). These seven women toured the United States displaying their floor-length tresses, and sold products that would give every woman a flowing cascade of hair. It seems only appropriate that the sisters came from Niagara Falls, New York. Today, just as then, many dollars are spent worldwide on haircuts, hair care products, hair transplants, and hair removal. In our own right, we inhabitants of the modern world have continued this obsession with hair.

Fig. 3.4. Photograph of the seven Sutherland sisters, c. 1890. *Photo courtesy of Rapunzel's Delight.*

By the end of the twentieth century, nineteenth century hair work was finally beginning to be understood and appreciated. For most of the twentieth century, hair work was maligned by being associated solely with death and grief and was lumped into the category of "funereal art." This misconception created a negative prejudice and led to the destruction of many cherished and beautiful examples of hair art. In this author's experience of collecting and restoring nineteenth century hair work, the majority of it is dedicated to the celebration of friendship, romance, the family, and life.

All in the Family

The preponderance of hair work created during the Victorian age was done in the nature of a family tree or to honor a group of persons who were living at the time. Such a group is honored in this marvelous dome (Fig. 3.5) that contains an espaliered tree of hair flowers with a heart-shaped engraved plaque that reads:

> *Primitive Methodist Society*
> *This tree contains hair of*
> *the present Ministers, Local Preachers,*
> *and Sunday School Teachers,*
> *of the above society*
> *Chester,*
> *1st June,*
> *1864.* (Fig. 3.6)

Not only does this dome have wonderful documentation, it also came from an interesting locale: Nassau in the Bahamas, where it had been in a collection that previously originated in the United States.

Fig. 3.5. Dome containing an espaliered tree of hair work flowers from the Primitive Methodist Society, June 1, 1864.

Fig. 3.6. Detail of Fig. 3.5.

Fig. 3.7. Lyre-shaped hair work sculpture with hair work flowers made from thirteen family members, c. 1870.

As a collector the goal is to find the unusual. Upon rare occasion there is the added bonus of an unexpected surprise. The next dome was first seen in a small print ad in the Newtown Bee, a weekly antiques newspaper. It was being auctioned in upstate New York, where there were a few examples of domes being sold but this one was most desirable, with the execution of the hair work being done in a lyre-shaped motif (Fig. 3.7). It was described over the phone as having small numbered paper tags sewn to the delicate hair flowers (Fig. 3.9), once again indicating a group or family that donated their locks. Realizing such a prize should not be entrusted to UPS, the author chose to bid in person and was successful. After collecting the dome it was time to start the 200+ mile trek home. The next day, the author lifted the glass dome and the hair work contents and there it was – a piece of folded yellowed graph paper with the names of all whose hair was gathered to create such a wonderful family record.

Fig. 3.8. Detail of Fig. 3.7.

1.
2. Mother's
3. Pa's
4. Mother's & Pa's
5. " "
6. Joshua's
7. "
8. "
9. Edith's
10. "
11. "
12. Albert's
13. Harrison's & Elva's
14. Grandmother Littlefield's
15. Aunt Hulda's
16. Uncle Alvin Macumber's
17. James Macumber's
18. Chandler "
19. Joseph "

Fig. 3.9. Detail of Fig. 3.7.

The thirteen members of this family, from the gray hair of Grandmother Littlefield to the pale blonde towhead, Edith, are represented in this beautifully and lovingly done example of nineteenth century sentimentality.

Fig. 3.10. Hair wreath created by Amy Ida Williams from her own hair, plus that of 52 family members and her pet pony "Pollie," c. 1882.

Provenance is one of the things most desired by collectors. It can be the added bonus to an item such as this hair work wreath in an oval shadow box (Fig. 3.10). The wreath was the most frequently chosen form for nineteenth century hair work in America (Fig. 3.11). When purchased via phone bid from a southeastern Pennsylvania auction house, the author had no idea what treasure lay hidden behind the wooden backboard. There, folded in quarters, was the original key or diagram drawn by the hair artist, Amy Ida Williams, herself (Fig. 3.12). As indicated by the date (1882), created "from the combings" of her own hair, the piece required one year to make. Amy collected hair from fifty three family members, all of whom are listed on the diagram. When examining the hair flowers the author noticed two simple ones in jet black hair. After referring to the key, it was noted that these were made from the mane of her pet pony, "Pollie" (Fig. 3.13).

Hair Wreath

Fig. 3.11. Suggestion for making a wreath of hair flowers from *Ladies Fancy Work*, 1876.

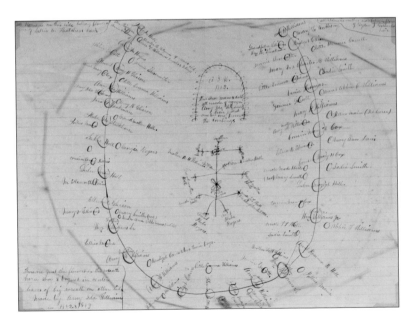

Fig. 3.12. Detail of Fig. 3.10.

Fig. 3.13. Detail of Fig. 3.10. Hair work flower made from "Pollie's" mane.

Mary Van Wyck is commemorated by this lyre-shaped hair work given to her by her class in 1872 (Fig. 3.14). At the top of the lyre above all the names is the inscription "Hair work executed by Isabella Heath," who may have been one of Mary's friends or a prize pupil (Fig. 3.15).

Another documented shadow box of unusual design is this large bouquet of hair flowers emanating from a cornucopia or tussy mussy (Figs. 3.16 and

3.17). The skill required to appliqué the delicate bands of hair work onto the upturned shape is remarkable. This piece is signed on the back, *Made by Mrs. William J. Smith 1860-1861 at Brookline N. H..* It was purchased sight unseen from a dealer friend of the author who phoned one day from New England and said, "There is a framed hair work here in an antique coop that I think you might like." His perception proved to be correct!

Fig. 3.14. Lyre-shaped hair wreath "presented to Mary Van Wyck, by her class, Jan. 1ˢᵗ, 1872."

Fig. 3.15. Detail of Fig. 3.14.

Fig. 3.17. Detail of Fig. 3.16.

Fig. 3.16. Hair work tussy mussy of hair work flowers "Made by Mrs. William J. Smith 1860-1861 at Brookline N.H." in gilt gesso oval frame.

As with most objects created by artists, the signature tends to give it importance and validity. Mentioned previously, the most desirable works of hair art are those which have a key or listing of the donors. It is an even rarer occurrence when a photograph or photographs are included in the composition, as shown in this hair wreath which surrounds a six by eight inch ambrotype of three people (Fig. 3.18). This technique involved the application of a solution or collodion to a piece of glass onto which the image/portrait was exposed creating a positive image. When photography was in its infancy, long periods of exposure time were required. This meant that the subjects had to remain motionless and holding a smile was generally not an option (Fig. 3.19).

A further example of juxtaposing hair work with photographic images is this incredible rectangular wreath of hair flowers purchased from an estate in Rhode Island (Fig. 3.20). If the rectangular shape of the hair wreath is not unusual enough, within its confines one finds eighteen daguerreotypes of those whose hair was graciously donated.

Fig. 3.19.
Detail of Fig. 3.18.

Fig. 3.18. Wreath of hair flowers with ambrotype photograph depicting three people in gilt frame, c. 1860.

Fig. 3.20. Rectangular wreath of hair work flowers surrounding eighteen daguerreotypes of family members in walnut frame, c. 1860s. *Photo courtesy of David Klutho.*

In Memoriam

Up until recently in modern times, there was a preoccupation with death. Death came early, openly, and life expectancies were short. Mourning customs had been practiced for centuries in western civilization, but it was during the nineteenth century that it became an art form. On December 14, 1861, Queen Victoria's husband, Prince Albert, died. The queen was devastated and withdrew from all public life. She wore her widow weeds for the next forty years. At the queen's request, Albert's clothing and toilet was laid out every morning wherever she was in residence. This carte de visite (Fig. 3.21), entitled, *"A Nation Mourns The Loss,"* depicts Victoria and her nine children in full mourning, with a portrait of Albert behind her. Albert's portrait, along with a lock of his hair, accompanied the queen on all of her travels and was placed on the pillow next to hers every night. She never fully recovered from Albert's death.

Fig. 3.21. Carte de visite depicting Queen Victoria and her nine children mourning the death of Prince Albert, "A Nation Mourns the Loss," c. 1862.

There is a large body of hair work that represents the memory of a lost loved one, but most often there is some inscription or symbols associated with death. These symbols may take the form of a willow tree, an inverted torch, or a complete cemetery scene (Fig. 3.22). Here the death of a young French woman, Sophie Henri, is memorialized under a glass dome. Every part of the scene that is dark brown (black) in color was done with the hair of the lovely girl pictured in the accompanying black-edged cart-de-visite photograph, originally found under the dome (Fig. 3.23). The cross, the willow tree, clumps of grass, and edging of the tomb were achieved by a technique known as cut or palette-work (which will be discussed later in this chapter). Locks of hair were coated in a gum-like mucilage, curled, and arranged in paper planters to suggest ferns. The papier mâché ground and the tree trunks are covered in finely chopped hair. There is an inscription penned on the tomb, *"Souvenir de Sophie Henri agee de 21 ans: decedee la 9 Juillet 1887"* (In Memory of Sophie Henri 21 years old deceased July 9 1887) (Fig. 3.24). Darlene Tsavaras of Things Gone by Antiques purchased this incredible piece

in France for the author. The story that accompanies it is that Sophie's family took her shorn tresses to Carmelite nuns who created the memorial as a means of supporting their convent. Another hair work memorial "dome story" was told to this author by an avid collector of Victoriana, who saw a rather short but elongated oval dome containing not only a hearse created from the deceased hair, but also a pair of cockaded horses pulling that were also made of hair. Its whereabouts remains unknown.

Fig. 3.23. Detail of Fig. 3.22.

Fig. 3.24. Detail of Fig. 3.22.

Fig. 3.22. French cemetery scene done in the hair of the deceased, (translated) "In Memory of Sophie Henri, 21 years old, deceased July 9. 1887."

The French were responsible for a multitude of hair memorials that spanned the entire nineteenth century. Many times they were presented as cemetery scenes similar to the domed example above, but they were also displayed as wall pieces in black oval frames with convex (domed) glass covering the fragile hair work (Fig. 3.25). There were so many produced that an entire chapter could be devoted to this form alone. The example illustrated here shows the before-mentioned palette work techniques so commonly used, with great attention to detail in the branches of the willow tree, the cast iron fence, and grass in the foreground. The horizon line is comprised of trees made from what was called "masticated" (chewed/ cut) hair taken from the deceased, a young woman, (trans.) "Madame J.C. Goethals wife of Monsieur Jules Carette, born the 9th of September 1842; died the 5th of May 1878 (Fig. 3.26).

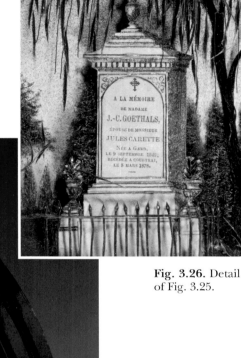

Fig. 3.26. Detail of Fig. 3.25.

Fig. 3.25. French hair work cemetery scene memorial in black oval frame commemorating the death of "Madame J.C. Goethals 1842-1878."

Fig. 3.27.
French hair
work memorial
done in curled
and palette work
blonde hair
with the name,
"Alexandre
Rimbault, at age
18 months.".

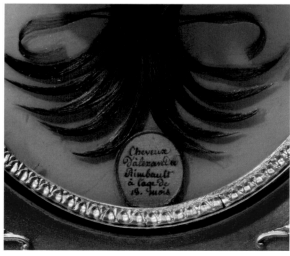

Fig. 3.28. Detail of Fig. 3.27.

Whether as a memorial or not, this elegant French work comprised of a bouquet of blonde curls makes a striking presentation (Fig. 3.27). Beneath the bound curls is a small paper plaque with the inscription, *"Cheveux d'alexandre Rimbault a l'âge de 18 Mois"* (Hair of Alexander Rimbault at the age of 18 months) (Fig. 3.28). Was Alexander the victim of the childhood mortality that was prevalent during the era, or is this a souvenir of his first haircut? Memorializing the loss of a child was common and for those who could afford it, a figure carved in marble was the ultimate expression, as seen in this statue attributed to William Henry Rinehart (1825-1874) (Fig. 3.29). Rinehart, a Maryland native, apprenticed as a stone-cutter before studying sculpture in 1844 at the Maryland Institute of Art. In 1855 he went to Italy to further his studies and became one of the foremost neoclassical sculptors of his day. Memorials of children became a specialty of his and other examples can be found at Belmont Plantation in Nashville, Tennessee, and the Maryland State Archives.

Another sculpture created in Parian porcelain, this *Death Mask of an Unknown Lady* c. 1870, also conveys the idea of eternal sleep (Fig. 3.30).

Fig. 3.29. Life-size white marble sculpture presented as a memorial to a deceased child, attributed to American sculptor, William Henry Rinehart (1825-1874), c. 1860.

Fig. 3.30. Sculpture in Parian porcelain depicting a post mortem portrait of a woman, English, maker unknown, c.1870.

A dome with an American origin may also fall into the category of what the French call a "souvenir," or remembrance, as it consists of a bouquet of multi-colored hair flowers placed in a porcelain vase. Adhered to each of the flowers is a tiny numbered tab (Figs. 3.31 and 3.32) that corresponds to the inscription glued to the underside of the dome's base. It is written:

In Memory of the Family of Charles Davison
Hair marked No 1. Charles Davison
No 2. Meg Davison
No 3. Gertrude Davison
No 4. Walter Davison
The remaining hair not marked Bessie Davison
Work done by Mrs. C.B. Stoltz
Prospect Plains, N.J.

Fig. 3.32. Detail of Fig. 3.31.

Fig. 3.31. Bouquet of hair work flowers with numbered tags in porcelain vase with paper label under the base indicating five members of the Charles Davison family, c. 1865.

Fig. 3.33. Pair of hair work willow trees with black ribbons, c. 1880. *Photo courtesy of David Klutho.*

Fig. 3.34. American memorial cemetery scene exhibiting palette work, gimp, and masticated hair work techniques, c. 1870.

The word memory in this case may suggest that either this hair work represents a piece of genealogy or the tragic loss of the five members of the Davison family. When one sees the symbols mentioned above, such as a hair work willow tree (Fig. 3.33) or the cemetery scene done in this American example (Fig. 3.34), the answer is clear. Another tell-tale sign indicating a memorial piece is the use of only one color of hair, albeit the deceased.

Techniques of Creating Hair Art

The two techniques used for creating the hair work examples in this chapter are cut or palette work and gimp work. The first, palette work was illustrated in *Godey's* February 1851 issue (Fig. 3.35). The instructions guide the novice hair artist through a series of steps that involve the creation of small "sheets" of hair.

> *For working these, ivory, such as miniature painters use, short lengths of hair, viz: from two to four inches, and gum dragon, are all the materials required, with the exception of a piece of thread. For tools, a fine-edged penknife, a very delicate pair of scissors with fine sharp points, a couple of fine camel's-hair pencils, a fine stiletto or long pin, and a palette* (of glass or marble) *are all that are needful.*

The cleaned and dried shock of hair was flattened onto the piece of glass with no overlapping of the strands. The gum dragon or mucilage was applied to the entire piece and dried thus creating a sheet. Templates of the petals and leaves from the intended design were placed on this and cut out, always on the bias, with a very sharp penknife or scissors.

Once all of the elements were cut out, the assembly or gluing onto the ivory or milk glass could begin. A suitable glass-covered frame would protect the delicate work, as seen in this example of palette work pansies that retains its original sketch in the oval leather case (Fig. 3.36). Numbers are indicated on the sketch but unfortunately a key is not present. Palette work was the technique of choice for the multitudes of hair work brooches created in the nineteenth century with a popular motif being the Prince of Wales plumes (Fig. 3.37).

Group Carnations.

Fig. 3.35. Suggestion of a design for a group of carnations to be done using the palette work technique, c. 1851, *Godey's Lady's Book.*

Prince's Feather.

Fig. 3.37. Prince's Feather or "Prince of Wales" design for palette work technique, c. 1851, *Godey's Lady's Book.*

Fig. 3.36. Oval leather case containing a floral hair work design of pansies in the palette work technique with original numbered drawing/key, c. 1855.

The second technique used by the hair artist was called gimp work. This predominately was used to create three dimensional flowers and objects in hair that would be displayed under shades or in shadow boxes. The technique involved making a chain or "gimp" of tiny loops of hair on thin wire (Fig. 3.38). All that was required were long strands of various colored hair, wire, and a selection of needles or rods in varying thicknesses. The artist looped the hair over the needle as they twisted the wire beneath it. Once a length was achieved it could be formed into the shape of a single petal or leaf (Fig. 3.39). In this author's opinion, this is one of the most unappreciated forms of parlor arts. Upon close examination of a hair wreath created in gimp work one realizes the virtuosity of the hair artist.

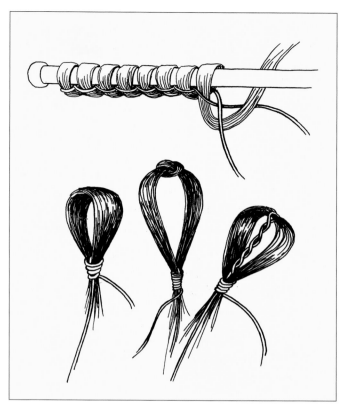

Fig. 3.38. Illustration of "gimp" hair work techniques.

Fig. 3.39. Detail of a "gimp" hair work flower, c. 1860s.

With a rather limited or monochromatic palette in the colors of hair the artist must combine a variety of patterns of the looped hair to create interest. This is evident in this domed hair work bouquet that is arranged in a Parian porcelain hand vase (Fig. 3.40). Exhibiting various shades of hair and wiring patterns a matched pair of domes filled with hair work flowers are a rarity (Fig. 3.41). What is even rarer is the fact that they were purchased separately from different sources. Forms that are something other than flowers such as a hovering butterfly and a small bird perched on top of this next arrangement are most desirable (Fig. 3.42 to 3.44). Most hair work flowers done in the gimp technique have a stylized appearance. This is not the case with this bouquet in a gilt oval shadow box purchased from an estate on Boston's north shore (Fig. 3.45). The flowers are rendered realistically with most garden varieties being readily identified as geraniums, bells of Ireland, fuchsias, lilies, and bleeding hearts.

Fig. 3.40. Bouquet of hair work flowers arranged in a Parian porcelain hand vase. c. 1860.

Fig. 3.41. Very rare matched pair of hair work flower arrangements in domes, c. 1870.

Fig. 3.43. Detail of Fig. 3.42.   **Fig. 3.44.** Detail of Fig. 3.42.

Fig. 3.42. A bouquet of hair work flowers done in a folk art manner including a butterfly and a bird, c. 1855, presented in a late 18th century green glass vase.

Fig. 3.45. Naturalistic bouquet of hair work flowers purchased from a Boston North Shore Estate, c. 1860.

The Long and the Short of It

The beginning of the twentieth century brought an end to many things. Thanks to Henry Ford and the Wright Brothers, man's ability to travel from one point to another took on an entirely new meaning. World War I, "The War to End All Wars," changed the face of Europe. Revolutions occurred in Czarist Russia, kings fell in Austria and in other parts of Eastern Europe, and, on the domestic level, the Women's Suffrage Movement grew in America and abroad. The role of women in society was changing drastically and the outcry for independence and the vote was heard around the world. No longer was the image of a fragile hothouse plant accepted by the modern woman. As women dispensed with the antiquated notions of the past, they did the same with their long tresses. "The Bob" was said to be started in 1915 by dancer Irene Castle. This blunt cut revolutionized hair fashion and was symbolic of independent young women of the new century. The embodiment of the new age was "The It Girl" herself, Clara Bow (Fig. 3.46), who flaunted more than her bobbed hair on the silver screen. The art of hair work met its end as well. The Jazz Age had no time for parlor pastimes, and the idea of memorializing one's hair went out of fashion with The Gibson Girl.

Fig. 3.46. Photograph of Clara Bow, "The It Girl," c. 1920.

4
NATURE CONTAINED
"BIRDS, DOGS, FROGS, AND MONKEYS TOO!"

Fig. 4.1. Young athlete with bird domes, English, c. 1885.

Fig. 4.2. *Still life with Bird Dome*, oil on canvas, John Bulloch Souter (Scottish) 1890-1972, c. early 20th century.

Historically Speaking

The word taxidermy is derived from the Latin root "taxi" (moving/to move) and "derma" (skin). Over six hundred years ago, during the age of enlightenment in western civilization, man began not only to explore but to question the world around him. Exploration of new worlds created a fascination, almost an obsession, with all forms of life that theretofore had not been seen by Europeans. Not only were the stories of these new-found creatures brought back from the explorations, in many cases the creatures themselves were brought. Many of these were destined to perish on the long voyage home, so the preserving of skins or carcasses became a necessity. Man had developed techniques for tanning or preserving animal hides over the millennia. But now the concept had shifted from that of a functional purpose to that of scientific

or decorative. One of the illustrative tales involved the beautiful greater bird of paradise (Fig. 4.3) from the island of New Guinea. The scientific name of that bird is *Paradisea apoda* or the "footless" bird of paradise. When the first skins arrived in Europe during the sixteenth century, none of the specimens had their feet attached, so it was told that this bird was so beautiful and mystical that it spent its entire life in flight, never touching a branch or the ground. Discovered and classified in the late nineteenth century, this male blue bird of paradise (*Paradisea rudolphi*), was named for the ill-fated Crown Prince Rudolf of Austria. This rare bird was mounted in his mating display pose, which is upside down (Fig. 4.4 and 4.5).

Fig. 4.3. *Paradisea apoda*, print, 7 x 10 inches, c. 19th century.

Fig. 4.4. Blue bird of paradise, *Paradisea rudolphi*, c. 1900.

Fig. 4.5. Detail of Fig. 4.4.

The focus of this book is the Victorian age or nineteenth century, and this chapter is by no means an attempt to be a treatise on the history of taxidermy. The focus here is on how the Victorians welcomed taxidermy into their everyday lives and how it developed into an industry the likes of which had never been seen and never will again. And nowhere was this more the case than in Great Britain. Every town, hamlet or village had a resident taxidermist, as seen in this illustration of Shaw's taxidermy shop in Shrewsbury (Fig. 4.6). (Note the row of domed specimens in the windows). Arthur Rogers of Nottingham displayed a varied selection of domed taxidermy in their shop window as well (Fig. 4.7). In this book's bibliography there are listed several excellent references to British taxidermy such, as *The History of British Taxidermy* by Christopher Frost. Another group of entries are those written by Dr. Pat Morris of London, a professor emeritus of zoology at London University, who has dedicated a large part of his life to the why, when, and wherefore of the art and history of taxidermy. It is within these books you will find the full story of taxidermy in not only Great Britain, but also in Europe, America, and faraway places such as India.

Fig. 4.7. Arthur Rogers taxidermy shop, Nottingham, Nottinghamshire, c. 1900. *Photo courtesy of P. Morris.*

Fig. 4.6. Henry Shaw's Taxidermy Shop, Shrewsbury, Shropshire, c. 1896. *Photo courtesy of Shropshire Archives.*

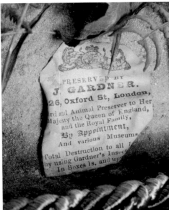

Fig. 4.9. Detail of Fig. 4.8.

PRESERVED BY
J. GARDNER.
26, Oxford St, London,
Bird and Animal Preserver to Her
Majesty the Queen of England,
and the Royal Family,
By Appointment,
And various Museums

Total Destruction to all
by using Gardner's Insec
In Boxes 1s, and up

Fig. 4.10. Detail of Fig. 4.8.

Fig. 4.8. Pair of male resplendent quetzals, etc., James Gardner, c. 1890.

Rule Britannia: 19th Century British Taxidermy

The center of British taxidermy was London, where rows of taxidermist shops lined such areas as Oxford St. One of the most renowned taxidermists of Oxford Street was James Gardner, who created this magnificent three foot high dome of two male resplendent quetzals accompanied by a few other tropical friends (Fig. 4.8). As indicated by the label behind the arrangement (Figs. 4.9 and 4.10), Gardner received patronage from the royal family, with the Queen of England (Victoria) herself cited. Some other names

Fig. 4.13. Label of Edward Gerrard & Sons, taxidermist. *Photo courtesy of P. Morris.*

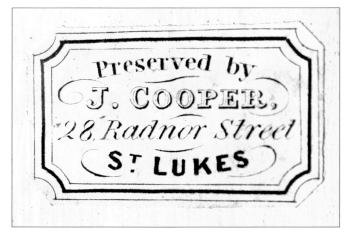

Fig. 4.11. Label of J. Cooper, taxidermist. *Photo courtesy of P. Morris.*

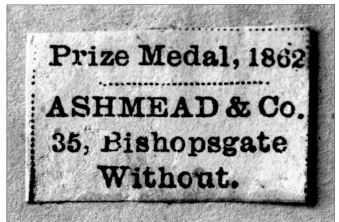

Fig. 4.14. Label of Ashmead & Co., taxidermist. *Photo courtesy of P. Morris.*

Fig. 4.12. Label of Leadbeater & Son, taxidermist. *Photo courtesy of P. Morris.*

of London taxidermists from this period are John Gould, John Cooper & Sons (Fig. 4.11), Leadbeater & Son (Fig. 4.12), Edward Gerrard & Sons (Fig. 4.13), and George Ashmead & Co,=. (Fig. 4.14). As one can see, these were family businesses that survived for decades. One of the most preeminent families whose firm spanned the nineteenth and twentieth centuries was the Ward family, consisting of Henry and his sons, Edwin and Rowland.

Henry Ward (1812-1878) was associated with America's most famous naturalist, John James Audubon, and accompanied him as a preserver of specimens during one of Audubon's expeditions to Florida. It is presumed they met in London in 1831. Ward developed his own taxidermy business in London at 2 Vere St. in 1857, and remained there until his death in 1878. His sons, trained by him, established their own taxidermy shops independently. They were every bit the artist that their father was. This author has developed his own theory regarding the influence of the ornithological prints created by Audubon and the way in which bird specimens came to be presented under glass. Prior to the nineteenth century, natural history specimens were presented in a static "rigor mortis"-like manner with very little consideration for realism and animation. Audubon revolutionized the art of representing natural history in two dimensions. His birds are depicted in very excited poses with wings spread, beaks open, and interacting in dramatic scenarios. In order to sketch these animated poses, the specimens had to be wired and mounted in a way that heretofore had not been done. The transference from a two-dimensional print to a three-dimensional arrangement is well illustrated by this exquisite walnut fire screen created by Henry Ward (Fig. 4.15). It bears his label inside the ornately carved Rococo-style case (Fig. 4.16). The interior is filled with brilliantly colored exotic birds to suggest that a slice of the rainforest canopy has been preserved with all of its excitement and diversity. Examples such as this by Henry Ward are not common and are generally of excellent quality.

Fig. 4.15. Walnut Rococo Revival-style fire screen by Henry Ward, c. 1857-78. *Photo courtesy of Clevedon Salerooms, Somerset, U.K.*

Fig. 4.16. Detail of Fig. 4.15.

Fig. 4.17. Exotic bird dome by James Gardner, c. 1880.

James Gardner, mentioned above, captured this drama under domes. Although Gardner was a general taxidermist who advertised himself as a "bird, animal, and fish preserver," he excelled at creating arrangements of what was commonly referred to as "foreign" birds, such as this large dome (Fig. 4.17). It contains an ecstatic rainbow lory at the top, as well as a rare, male green broadbill with wings spread at the bottom as his mate looks on with disinterest (Fig. 4.18). In most cases, these tropical bird domes do not contain birds from a specific region of the world. In the nineteenth century it was said that the sun never

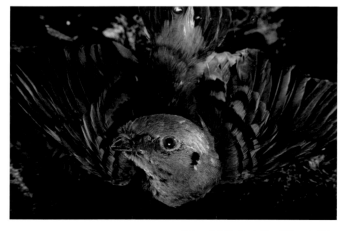

Fig. 4.18. Detail of Fig. 4.17.

set on the British Empire. Specimens of birds from every corner of the globe poured into London, so the taxidermists had an enormous selection from which to choose. With that being the case, aesthetics, in many instances, overruled geographic accuracy. A non-labeled example is this giant oval dome containing a trio of lesser birds of paradise arranged in a Ziegfield Follies manner, with smaller birds from the Americas and Asia (Fig. 4.19). Another oval dome shows a group of South American and Caribbean birds, including some rare species of hummingbirds such as the Jamaican streamer tail and the booted spatula-tailed in the upper left (Figs. 4.20 to 4.23). The center bird is a king bird of paradise from New Guinea.

Fig. 4.19. A large oval dome of exotic birds including lesser birds of paradise, c. 1880.

Fig 4.20. Dome of mixed exotic birds, English, c. 1870.

Fig. 4.21. Detail of Fig. 4.20. A racket-tailed hummingbird.

Fig. 4.22. Detail of Fig. 4.20. A tail wire plume of the king bird of paradise.

Fig. 4.23. Detail of Fig. 4.20. King bird of paradise.

Fig. 4.24. A large oval dome of Australian birds by James Gardner, c. 1875.

There were also domes that focused on indigenous species, such as this labeled example by Gardner containing a wide variety of Australian birds (Fig. 4.24). Here we see everything from gaudy parrots, the rare regent honeyeater, and a wompoo dove to small, gem-like fairy wrens. This example was found in a castle in Inverness, Scotland. The unusually exotic is best illustrated in this very tall and narrow oval dome featuring an Amazonian umbrella bird, with his pompadour crest that has earned him the nickname "Elvis" (Fig. 4.25). He has a supporting cast of brilliant hummingbirds and tanagers that come from the rainforests of Central and South

Fig. 4.25. A tall narrow dome with an Amazonian umbrellabird, c. 1870.

Fig. 4.26. Mixed exotic bird dome, attributed to Williams & Sons, Dublin, Ireland, c. late 19th century.

America. Though not labeled, the next dome has a beautifully composed array of South American species (Fig. 4.26), such as the neon blue spangled cotinga (Fig. 4.27), the fiery Guianan red cotinga (Fig. 4.28), and the rarely seen royal flycatcher, with its outrageous crest (Fig. 4.29). This artistically executed dome, purchased from a sale in Dublin, Ireland, could be attributed to Williams & Son, who included in their label (Fig. 4.30), *"Glass shades and cases artistically arranged."*

Fig. 4.27. Detail of Fig. 4.26. A spangled cotinga.

Fig. 4.28. Detail of Fig. 4.26. A Guianan red cotinga.

Fig. 4.30. Label of Williams & Son, taxidermist, Dublin, Ireland, c. 19th century.

Fig. 4.29. Detail of Fig. 4.26. A royal flycatcher.

A superb presentation of a geographically focused bird dome is this gargantuan oval dome that stands three-and-one-half feet high and over two feet wide (Fig. 4.31). The theme is the island of New Guinea, with many species of birds of paradise being represented. There are three Count Raggianas, two magnificent birds of paradise, a magnificent riflebird (Fig. 4.32), and a king bird of paradise, all in their mating display mode. Another component sometimes found in exotic bird domes is colorful, preserved insects. They add to the beauty of the jungle scene depicted. The insects in this dome are found in New Guinea as well (Figs. 4.33 and 4.34).

Fig. 4.31. A 42 inch high dome containing birds of paradise and insects native to Papua, New Guinea, c. late 19th century.

Fig. 4.32. Detail of Fig. 4.31, magnificent riflebird, *Ptiloris magnificus*, Papua, New Guinea.

Fig. 4.33. Detail of Fig. 3.31, beetle, *Rosenbergia straussi*, Papua, New Guinea.

Fig. 4.34. Detail of Fig. 4.31, birdwing butterfly, *Ornithoptera paradisea*, Papua, New Guinea.

Fig. 4.35. Rococo Revival parlor with
laminated rosewood furniture by
John Henry Belter, c. 1850-1860, and
collection of 19th century glass domes.

Larger birds of all species were presented under domes, whether in pairs such as these Livingstone's turacos from equatorial Africa (Fig. 4.36), or as single specimens, seen here in this Victoria crowned pigeon (Fig. 4.37). An elegant male western tragopan from the Himalayas, with his mating wattle and horns in full display (Figs. 4.38 and 4.39), occupies this tall dome by Gardner with an interior gilt plateau.

Fig. 4.36. A pair of Livingstone's turacos, c. 1885.

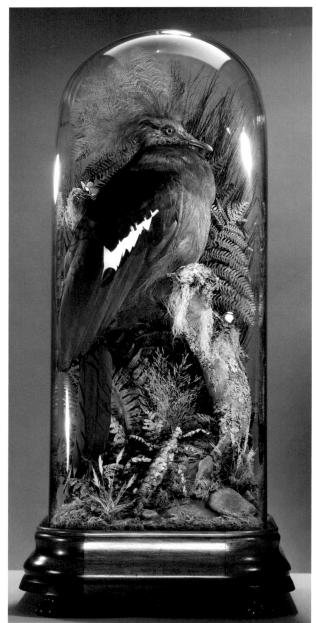

Fig. 4.37. A Victoria crowned pigeon, c. 1870.

Fig. 4.39.
Detail of Fig. 4.38.

Fig. 4.38. Tragopan
pheasant by James
Gardner, c. 1880.

Stuffed birds under domes were not limited to tabletop display. One can find fine examples such as this wall mount half dome of hoopoes by Peter Spicer of Leamington (Fig. 4.40). Spicer was a highly skilled and prolific taxidermist and "naturalist," as indicated by the label (Fig. 4.41). He lived a long life (1839-1934) and included his sons, William and Gilbert, in the family business, which was started in 1798 by his great-grandfather and spanned three centuries. Small round glass domes were used for wall presentations, as seen in this charming little pair, which contain a hummingbird and a red legged honeycreeper (Figs. 4.42 and 4.43). Imperfect domes could be cut into cylindrical sections or rings of glass, which made ideal spaces in which birds could be displayed, such as these turquoise parakeets signed en verso by James Gardner in 1876 (Fig. 4.44). A similar example is a golden oriole (Fig. 4.45). Another form of wall mounted taxidermy is the oval frame

Fig. 4.40. Wall dome of hoopoes by Peter Spicer, Leamington, Warwickshire, late 19th century.

Fig. 4.41. Peter Spicer label, detail of Fig. 4.40.

Fig. 4.42. Wall dome with hummingbird, c. 1895.

Fig. 4.44. Wall dome of turquoise parakeets by James Gardner, c. 1876.

Fig. 4.43. Wall dome with red-legged honeycreeper, c. 1895.

Fig. 4.45. Wall dome with golden oriole, c. 1880.

with a domed piece of glass. This gilt and ebonized frame containing colorful tanagers (Fig. 4.46) proves what a lovely option this could be. A pair of oval cases suitable for the parlor was purchased on Portobello Road (Fig. 4.47). The gilded gesso frames simulate branches and ivy leaves in a style that could be defined as "elegant rustic." Hidden within the groundwork is a printed label that reads, *"Medal Awarded, Ralph Allder, Taxidermist etc., Bartholomew St., Newbury"* which is located in the county of Berkshire, Great Britain (Fig. 4.48). In all of these cases, the background panel is painted in an opaque, water-based tempera paint to simulate a sunset, which provides a romantic backdrop for the groundwork and branches. This painting of the back panel is typical of British examples.

Fig. 4.46. Wall dome with tanagers (one of a pair), c. 1885.

Fig. 4.47. Gilt oval shadow box with exotic birds (one of a pair) by Ralph Allder, Newbury, Berkshire, c. 1870.

Fig. 4.48. Ralph Allder label, detail of Fig. 4.47.

There was a lot of inferior taxidermy produced commercially during the latter part of the nineteenth century, as indicated by the ready-made examples being offered in the Silber & Fleming Catalog published in London in 1880. Silber & Fleming offered an array of fancy goods such as china, silver, glassware, and arrangements of stuffed birds under glass shades (Fig. 4.49). These tend to be a hodgepodge of poorly mounted birds arranged on spindly branches with rather gaudily painted groundwork. They were created in great quantities using shortcuts in presenting the specimens, such as mounting the birds without legs and thereby eliminating that part of the wiring. Arrangements such as these became de rigueur in many middle-class Victorian parlors and have been classified by most writers on the subject of taxidermy as sub-standard and as having little or no merit other than being decorative. In fact, many of the incredible examples illustrated here are seen in a rather narrow view by some as being purely decorative and not of much scientific value. They were produced by some of the most skilled taxidermists and were sold as luxury items to the carriage trade with the most discriminating tastes. These wonderfully colorful and diverse exotic birds catch the viewer's eye and draw them in for closer inspection. The other argument for these decorative arrangements of birds is that, if their only purpose was to be that of decoration, why are so many of the birds labeled with small numbers at their feet that correspond to a key listing the species? Cannot one assume there was some educational value here as well?

The ultimate expression of artistry in decorative taxidermy under glass, as previously illustrated in the example by Henry Ward, is the bird fire screen, where not only the skills of the taxidermist reign supreme, but also those of the cabinetmaker. Over the centuries during the warmer months, when the fireplace was not in use, it was common practice to mask it with a fire screen, which in many cases exhibited the needle work artistry of the lady of the house. During the Victorian era it provided a place for ornithological masterpieces. The cases that housed the specimens reflected the design tastes of the decade in which they were produced whether they were in carved mahogany, gilt wood, or the more humble bamboo. Henry Ward's son Edwin created this piece in mahogany (Fig. 4.50). Inside near the bottom left hand corner is his

No. 3692   Nine Stuffed Birds, of bright plumage, under oval glass shade, fitted on black wooden stand ; extreme height about 20½ inches, length about 13½ inches, width about 7 inches

Fig. 4.49. Illustration from Silber & Fleming catalog, London, 1880. *Photo courtesy of © Victoria and Albert Museum, London.*

label that reads, *E. Ward 'Naturalist' 60 Wigmore Street, Cavendish Square London W* (Fig. 4.51). The label dates the piece between 1870, when he moved to this address, and 1879, the year of his retirement. Soon after retiring he emigrated to the United States where, in Pasadena, California, he had hopes of creating a natural history museum the likes of which he had admired in Washington, D.C. Advertisements were placed in the *Pasadena and Valley* newspaper during the 1880s (which can be viewed on microfiche at the Pasadena Chamber of Commerce Archives). Known as "General" Ward, he made the appeal for geological, archeological, zoological, and ornithological specimens. Due to over-speculation, his dream sadly never came to fruition and he died in America, broken and disappointed (Frost, p. 18).

Fig. 4.50. Mahogany fire screen with exotic birds by Edwin Ward, London, c. 1870.

Fig. 4.51. Edwin Ward label, detail of Fig. 4.50.

One example that surpasses the others is this magnificent fire screen attributed to Leadbeater & Son of London (Fig. 4.52). It stands over five feet tall and is constructed of ebonized wood with gilt ormolu trim. Housed in this glass aviary are fifty-two exotic specimens of fine quality, with a flamboyant Major Mitchell's cockatoo (Fig. 4.53) as the star, and a supporting cast of brilliant hummingbirds, tanagers, and parrots. Each bird has a tiny numbered tag glued to its branch that correlates to a key that is contained in a small drawer below, giving both the common and Latin names. It certainly lends credence to the provenance that it once graced one of the royal palaces.

Fig. 4.53. Detail of Fig. 4.52.

Fig. 4.52. Ebonized wood with gilt ormolu fire screen containing fifty two exotic birds, attributed to Leadbeater & Son, London, c. 1865.

Victorian parlors were often dark spaces due to heavy draperies and the poor lighting of the era. The use of gold leaf applied to moldings, picture frames, and furniture provided much needed reflective surfaces to enhance ambient light. The Rococo Revival in interior design during the mid-nineteenth century was referred to as "The Antique French," evoking the eras of Louis XIV to Louis XVI, when gilt wood furniture became highly desirable. The following two fire screens demonstrate this taste for all things French.

Ornately turned stiles joined by a similar stretcher on stout cabriole legs provide the frame for this case of South American birds (Fig. 4.54). A trio of orange and black troupials guards a nest in its center, as groupings of hummingbirds and manakins go about their business. It has on its underside a discreet label that simply says "Davy of Grimsby," which is located in Lincolnshire.

Fig. 4.54. Gilt wood fire screen containing exotic birds, by Davy of Grimsby, c. 1870.

Another gilded fire screen (Fig. 4.55) consists of a beautifully arched case topped by an applied shell, flower, and ribbon crest (Fig. 4.56). It contains a miniature aviary of various feathered gems and shimmering butterflies, portrayed in a frenzied state (Fig. 4.57). With its delicate moldings and graceful legs, it could have easily been found in the sitting room of Empress Eugenie or Marie Antoinette. As tastes in decoration changed during the 1880s and 1890s, motifs from the Rococo and Renaissance periods were replaced with those from the Far East. Artists and designers looked to Japan for their inspiration. Curved silhouettes and carved surfaces gave way to rectilinear forms and inlaid or incised ornamentation.

Fig. 4.55. Gilt wood fire screen in the Rococo Revival style containing exotic birds, English, c. 1855.

Fig. 4.56. Detail of (shell and flower crest) Fig. 4.55.

Fig. 4.57. Detail of Fig. 4.55.

A popular material for such furniture was bamboo, which was used in many forms including this fire screen done in the style popularized by Rowland Ward (1847-1912) (Fig. 4.59). A lighter, more minimalistic framework of ebonized bamboo supports a five-sided glass case that features specimens from Australia. Rowland, being the more successful of Henry Ward's sons, embodied the title of artist/taxidermist. After ten years of apprenticeship at his father's studio, he decided to create his own business (Fig. 4.60). What ensued over the next forty years can only be described as phenomenal. His list of clientele included royalty as well as some of the most renowned sportsmen of the era. No job or animal was too big for his studio. The innovative way in which he preserved and presented specimens was unprecedented. Throughout his life he continued to produce bronze sculptures, an inherent talent that is apparent in his own taxidermy work as well as all the items produced by his studio.

Fig. 4.58. American Rococo Revival mantle setting. The mantle is surmounted by an opulent oval mirror and by three pieces of Old Paris porcelain by Jacob Petit. The mantle is trimmed with a hand-beaded lambrequin.

Fig. 4.59. Extraordinary white marble parlor mantelpiece, c. 1855, serving as a backdrop for a Japanesque ebonized and gilt bamboo fire screen containing exotic birds attributed to Rowland Ward, c. 1885.

Fig. 4.60. Rowland Ward label, c. 1905. *Photo courtesy of P. Morris.*

Fig. 4.61. Vignette of a sideboard cabinet by Pottier & Stymus, New York, c. 1885, decorated with John Moyr Smith tiles and displaying a pair of Minton Aesthetic decorated moon vases and a monumental-sized exotic bird dome, presented in front of hand-blocked wallpaper by Zuber & Cie.

Fig. 4.62. Monumental-sized dome containing twenty seven exotic birds, English, c. 1880.

Made in America

The taste for stuffed birds under glass existed in America as well. The taxidermy industry of the nineteenth century in America did not exhibit the same decorative or artistic qualities of those abroad. Generally not as elaborate as their English and French counterparts, American bird domes were created in lesser quantities. There are several characteristics that differentiate the American bird dome from those made in Europe, the first being the tendency to use native species rather than foreign birds. Also, the use

of solid black glass eyes, rather than colored glass eyes with pupils, is common (the latter gives a more realistic expression). Another factor is the materials used in the groundwork, such as grasses and ferns that are indigenous to North America (groundwork is defined as the materials used to create the naturalistic setting in which the birds/specimens are presented). The tendency in America was to use wire armatures with applied excelsior and papier-mâché to create the central tree, rather than actual branches. Moreover, the general lack of realism of the scene depicted under the dome makes the American examples appear more rigid or static.

Fig. 4.63. An American taxidermist trade card, late 19th century.

This American method of displaying birds is illustrated in this thirty-inch high round dome that has an unusual elliptical profile (Fig. 4.64). In the forty years of looking at domes this author has seen very few domes that have this particular shape. It contains over three dozen birds arranged in a revolving formation around the central tree as an axis. One also finds a headless body of a native corn snake wrapped around the base of the tree. It was not uncommon in American bird domes to have an indigenous reptile or two included, such as preserved snakes and turtles.

Fig. 4.64. Large American elliptical-shaped bird dome, c. 1870.

Fig. 4.65. American bird dome containing exotic birds and family of quail in natural setting, c. 1875.

A very colorful and dramatic example is this large oval dome that shows a grouping of tropical birds in an artificial tree growing out of a papier-mâché rock formation, which supports a family of American quail (Fig. 4.65). Both mother and father and their brood of six chicks are busily exploring their setting (Fig. 4.66).

This mixing of foreign and local species is represented in the next smaller oval dome as well with an African gray parrot as the focal point (Fig. 4.67) Perhaps the parrot was someone's beloved pet, a topic we will discuss later in this chapter.

Fig. 4.66. Detail of Fig. 4.65.

Fig. 4.67. Oval American dome with African grey parrot, c. 1885.

It is rare to find a labeled American bird dome like the one illustrated here (Fig. 4.68). James M. Southwick created this dome of three American birds. As indicated by the label (Fig. 4.69), James Southwick was the proprietor of a "Natural History Store" located at "258 Westminster St. Providence Rhode Island, USA." Mr. Southwick provided all the necessary materials for the naturalist as well as the skills required for preserving and mounting mammals and birds. The birds in this dome each have a paper tag tied to the branch that reads, "10544, on branch", as, maybe, an indicator of inventory (Fig. 4.70).

Fig. 4.68. American bird dome by James M. Southwick, Providence, Rhode Island, c. late 19th century.

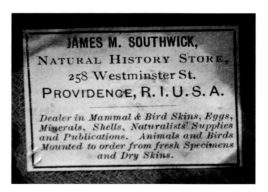

Fig. 4.69. James M. Southwick label, detail of Fig. 4.68.

Fig. 4.70. Detail of Fig. 4.68.

The Art of Taxidermy

Taxidermy was, and still is, considered an art form. The taxidermist not only uses skill in the preservation of the specimen, but also in its presentation. From the choice of glass eyes to the creation of groundwork, the elements and principles of design must be utilized. The goal is to capture a moment of time when the specimen was alive and do it in a realistic and convincing manner. Unfortunately many stuffed birds have an awkward, bug-eyed, stiff appearance. The taxidermist/artist who understands the anatomy, movements, and gestures of birds and mammals is most successful.

Montague Browne in his book, *Practical Taxidermy*, written in 1884, (Figs. 4.71 and 4.72) discusses the evolution of British taxidermy in the nineteenth century. The art of taxidermy was well represented at The Crystal Palace Exhibition of 1851, where taxidermists from all over Europe submitted their entries. No longer were the "stiff, gaunt, erect, and angular specimens of earlier times accepted or displayed. The teachings of these foreign exhibits opened the eyes of English taxidermists," (Browne, p. 16). The exhibition influenced them as well as others throughout the rest of the nineteenth century and into the present day.

Fig. 4.71. Cover of *Practical Taxidermy* by Montague Browne.

Fig. 4.72. Plate from *Practical Taxidermy* by Montague Browne.

Browne's book details all aspects of taxidermy art from decoying and trapping animals to the skinning of birds and mammals and the necessary tools required. Implements such as knives, scalpels, scissors, forceps, wire cutters, stuffing irons and materials are discussed in great detail (Figs. 4.73 to 4.75). The step-by-step procedure of skinning and preserving birds is covered with appropriate illustrations showing their skeletal structure (Fig. 4.76), as well as the process of preserving a starling, which culminates in the creation of a labeled study skin (Fig. 4.77) Browne also includes a chapter entitled "Preservative Soaps, Powders, Etc.," in which he gives the recipes of arsenical soaps. Arsenic was used extensively in the pigments of wall coverings and fabric dyes throughout the nineteenth century. Taxidermists created their own recipes for arsenical soap or paste that was to be spread throughout the interior of the skinned specimen. It was "the perfect drier of animal tissue, keeps all things free from attack of insects, and is easier to make than any other preparation." (Browne, p. 65) The main disadvantage, of course, was that it is poisonous.

Browne attributes the first use of arsenical soap to a Monsieur Becoeur during the 1770's and included the following recipe:

> **Becoeur's Arsenical Soap**
> *Camphor, 5 oz.*
> *Powdered arsenic, 2 lb.*
> *White soap, 2 lb.*
> *Salt of tartar, 12 oz.*
> *Lime in powder (or powdered chalk), 4 oz.*
>   (Browne, p.63)

Browne does not advocate arsenic as a preservative citing its many dangerous side effects and in its place suggests his own:

Browne's (non-poisonous) Preservative Soap
Whiting or chalk, 2 lb.
Chloride of lime, 2 oz.
Soft soap, 1 lb.
Tincture of musk, 1 oz.
   (Browne p. 68)

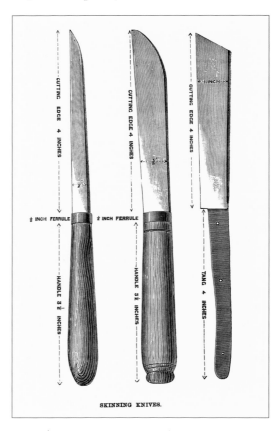

Fig. 4.73. Plate from *Practical Taxidermy* by Montague Browne.

Fig. 4.74. Plate from *Practical Taxidermy* by Montague Browne.

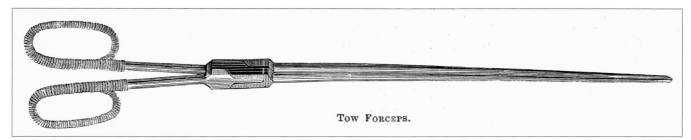

Fig. 4.75. Plate from *Practical Taxidermy* by Montague Browne.

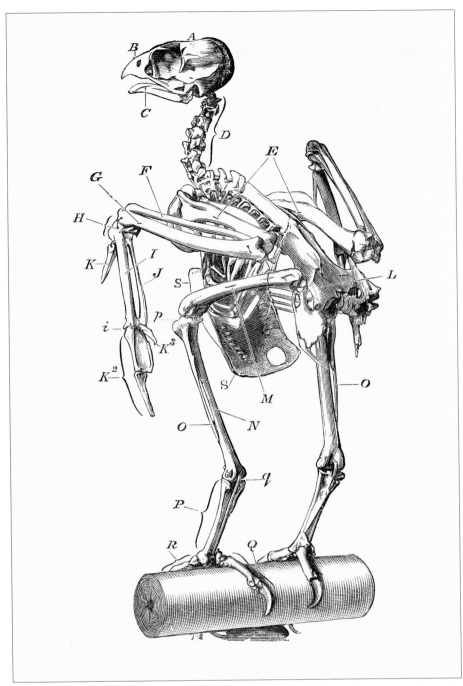

Fig. 4.76. Plate from *Practical Taxidermy* by Montague Browne.

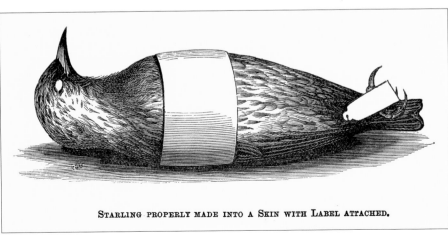

STARLING PROPERLY MADE INTO A SKIN WITH LABEL ATTACHED.

Fig. 4.77. Plate from *Practical Taxidermy* by Montague Browne.

After the bird's skin was sufficiently "preserved" the mounting process began. This included the stuffing of the cavity with tow and cotton and the insertion of wires to act as an armature. Interestingly an illustration that suggests the proper wiring of a bird specimen (Fig. 4.78) is found in the 1887 *"Ladies' Manual of Art or Profit and Pastime"* published in Philadelphia (Fig. 4.79). From the same manual comes this illustration of a Victorian lady scrutinizing a stuffed bird of paradise (Fig. 4.80). Perhaps she will add it to the tree of preserved birds on her work table. The beginning instructions read, "Take out the entrails; remove the skin with the greatest possible care; rub over the whole interior with arsenic (a deadly poison), etc." These directions are bit different from those used in the genteel art of making wax flowers. This indicates that taxidermists were not exclusively male; women also embraced taxidermy (Fig. 4.81). One such American woman was Martha Maxwell (1831-1881), posed in this photograph with her artist's palette and her rifle (Fig. 4.82). Unfortunately, labeled examples of taxidermy by women are few.

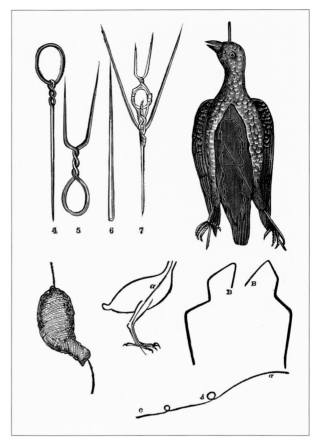

Fig. 4.78. Instructions for wiring a bird specimen, *Ladies' Manual of Art or Profit & Pastime,* 1887.

Fig. 4.79. Cover of *Ladies' Manual of Art or Profit & Pastime,* 1887.

AKE out the entrails; remove the skin with the greatest possible care; rub over the whole interior with arsenic, (a deadly poison;) put wires from the head to the legs to preserve the natural form, and stuff immediately with tow, wool, or the like. If allowed to dry after applying the arsenic, the skin becomes too stiff to handle.

Another, and, as we think, a better way for very small

Fig. 4.80. Illustration and instructions for stuffing a bird, *Ladies' Manual of Art. Photo courtesy of P. Morris.*

GABRIELLE RAY

Fig. 4.81. "Women embraced taxidermy."

Fig. 4.82. American taxidermist Martha Maxwell, c. 1875. *Photo courtesy of P. Morris.*

Not Just For the Birds

Victorian sentimentality and the idea of memorializing the dearly parted applied not only to humans. Man's faithful companion was also a subject to be preserved under glass domes. Nowhere was this more prevalent than England. A labeled example by James Gardner shows a regal Maltese in repose under an oval dome (Fig. 4.83). An alert Chihuahua with pricked ears relaxes on a bit of ingrain carpet under another deep oval dome (Fig. 4.84). She must have been dearly loved with her pink silk bow around her neck. This precious piece came from a vicarage estate sale in Hampshire. One of the most heart-wrenching domes is this terrier puppy (Fig. 4.85), which is actually Edwardian. He wears a tiny leather collar and stands on a patterned piece of wool fabric. His silver memorial plaque is inscribed, " LITTLE BOY" Born Sept 30th Died Dec 4th-1909 (Fig. 4.86).

Fig. 4.83. Maltese, labeled by James Gardner, c. late 19th century.

Fig. 4.84. Chihuahua, c. late 19th-early 20th century.

Fig. 4.85. "Little Boy" memorial dome of terrier puppy, c. 1909.

Fig. 4.86. Detail of Fig. 4.85.

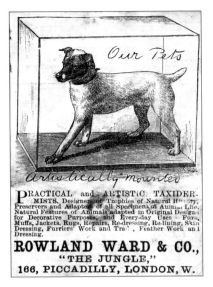

Pet dogs were "mounted artistically" in glass cases as advertised by Rowland Ward & Co. in the early 1900s (Fig. 4.87). One such beloved canine, a Yorkshire terrier, achieves a somewhat unsettling realistic appearance (Figs. 4.88 and 4.89) thanks to "E.H. Church, Bird & Animal Preserver, Midsomer Norton, Estimates Given."

This author experienced an incredible pet memorial in the shop owned by the beautiful and eccentric Emma Hawkins. Emma's shop on Westbourne Grove in London during the 1990s housed the most extraordinary collection of taxidermy and it was all for sale. The memorial consisted of a carved walnut glass-sided sarcophagus on a stepped base slightly over two feet square. Inside "slept" a miniature pinscher curled up within a wreath of strawflowers on a velvet cushion. The final touch was the name "Rosie" carved in the crest of the case. Living in regret, the author did not purchase it.

Fig. 4.87. Rowland Ward & Co. "Our pets artistically mounted" label, c. early 20th century. *Photo courtesy of P. Morris.*

Fig. 4.88. Yorkshire terrier in case by *E. H. Church, Bird & Animal Preserver, MidsomerNorton*, c. early 20th century.

Fig. 4.89. Detail of Fig. 4.88.

145

Some of the most unusual and puzzling examples of stuffed dogs are this pair of preserved "miniature" greyhounds (7 inches tall) under domes (Figs. 4.90 and 4.91). What makes them so intriguing is the modeling of their anatomical features. Each muscle and sinew is clearly defined (Fig. 4.92). After conferring with Dr. Pat Morris, who X-rayed another example, it was determined that the dog's bodies are composed of papier-mâché with the skins being meticulously fitted and stitched over the forms. Are these actual skins from stillborn puppies or are they something contrived by a skilled taxidermist?

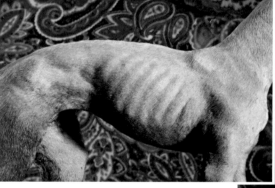

Fig. 4.92. Detail of Fig. 4.90.

Figs. 4.90 & 4.91. Miniature greyhound in dome, c. mid-19th century.

The next representation is unquestionably real. Here are two tiny pug puppies barely four inches high presented under a very low oval dome with a polished mahogany base (Fig. 4.93). They are mounted, one standing and one sitting, on a green velvet dais. All of their features from their tiny ears to their curled tails have been preserved (Figs. 4.94 and 4.95). This must have been a very special pair.

Fig. 4.93. Small mahogany based dome containing a pair of pug puppies, c. late 19ᵗʰ century.

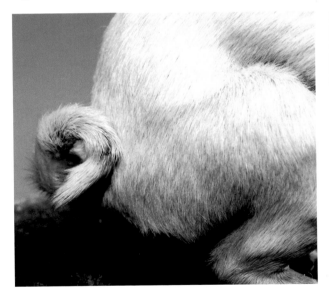

Fig. 4.94. Detail of Fig. 4.93.

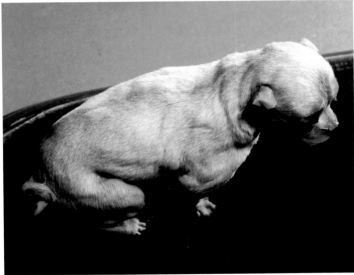

Fig. 4.95. Detail of Fig. 4.93.

Other pets were also stuffed and put in glass cases and under domes. A Guinea pig surrounded by small birds makes a charming presentation (Fig. 4.96). Pet parrots and canaries found their place in perpetuity under domes, as seen in this Amazon parrot in an excited state with mouth open perhaps saying hello or demanding a cracker (Fig. 4.97).

Another parrot under a glass dome, previously owned by the author, has a small printed card at its feet with the words "Forget Me Not" (Fig. 4.98). Additionally this specimen has its original metal label tacked onto its branch telling us it was worked by *M. J. Hofmann of 989 Gates Ave. Brooklyn, N. Y.* (Fig. 4.99).

Fig. 4.96. Small oval dome with Guinea pig and birds, c. 1890.

Fig. 4.98. Memorial dome containing pet parrot with "Forget Me Not" punch paper card, c. 1880. *From the collection of Leslie Orlowski.*

Fig. 4.99. Detail of Fig. 4.98.

Fig. 4.97. Large round dome with Amazon parrot in an excited state, c. 1880.

Anthropomorphic taxidermy

The next illustration depicts not the cuddly tabby or calico cat but rather a freak of nature (Fig. 4.102). Having eight legs this kitten was meant to be twins. It was part of the Potter Museum of Curiosities collection that was started by one of the most interesting taxidermists in the history of British taxidermy, Walter Potter (1835-1918). An entire book written by Dr. Pat Morris is devoted to the life of Mr. Potter and his museum. *Walter Potter and his Museum of Curious Taxidermy* is a must read for anyone interested in this subject. Mr. Potter put his own special twist on the art of taxidermy by including two-headed lambs and six-legged chickens, all casualties from local farms, in his museum. His small community of Bramber in Sussex provided a wealth of oddities and Mr. Potter set out to share them with the public at the cost of a small admission. The "Museum" formally opened its doors about 1880 (Fig. 4.103). Along with freaks of nature, Walter Potter's claim to fame was the creation of anthropomorphic scenes where preserved animals enacted the daily activities of humans, such as tea parties, croquet matches, and weddings (Fig. 4.104).

Following Potter's death in 1918, the museum was kept open by Potter's descendants until 1972. A new owner then moved the collection from its original site in Bramber. Over the next thirty years it changed

Fig. 4.102. Eight-legged kitten in dome from Mr. Potter's Museum of Curiosities, c. 19th century. *Photo courtesy of P. Morris.*

Fig. 4.103. Walter Potter in front of his museum at Bramber in Sussex, c. early 20th century. *Photo courtesy of P. Morris.*

Fig. 4.100. Anthropomorphic trade card, c. 1900.

Fig. 4.101. Anthropomorphic trade card, c. 1900.

Fig. 4.104. "The Kitten's Wedding" by Walter Potter, c. late 19th century. *Photo courtesy of P. Morris.*

hands and location several times until sadly, in 2003, the entire collection was sold at auction. The author was fortunate to acquire one of the more well-known items from the collection, the monkey riding the goat (Fig. 4.105). This infamous pair was united by Mr. Potter in 1870. According to legend, they were both mischievous beasts – the goat was a resident of Wiston Park in West Sussex, where no hedge or fence could keep him in. His final escape proved fatal when he met his end under a tradesman's team of horses. The monkey's habit of raiding a fruit shop in Shoreham caused his demise when the irritated owner threw a bucket of ice water over him and he died of shock. Mr. Potter decided these two rascals should be preserved with the monkey riding the goat to keep him in hand in perpetuity.

Fig. 4.105. "Monkey Riding the Goat" by Walter Potter, c. 1870.

Fig. 4.106. Illustration of frogs shaving by Hermann Ploucquet from the Crystal Palace Exhibition of 1851, London. *Photo courtesy of P. Morris.*

Anthropomorphic taxidermy was received with rave reviews when it was exhibited at The Crystal Palace Exhibition of 1851. After viewing an exhibit by Hermann Ploucquet of stuffed frogs engaged in comical activities such as shaving one another (Fig. 4.106) as well as "The Kittens at Tea-Miss Paulina Singing" (Fig. 4.107), even Queen Victoria was amused (Fig. 4.108). Ploucquet's entries of animal tableaux were most popular with visitors and were highly praised in several publications of the time.

Fig. 4.108. "Her Majesty The Queen Laughing," carte-de-visite. *Photo courtesy of Sotheby's Picture Library.*

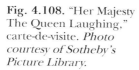

Fig. 4.107. Illustration of "The Kittens at Tea–Miss Paulina Singing" by Hermann Ploucquet at the Crystal Palace Exhibition of 1851, London. *Photo courtesy of P. Morris.*

Fig. 4.109. "Les Jeueurs des Billards" (the pool players), French, c. late 19ᵗʰ century.

Fig. 4.110. Detail of Fig. 4.109.

Fig. 4.111. Detail of Fig. 4.109.

Stuffed frogs involved in a variety of antics took residence under glass shades. In two French examples we find frogs playing a civilized game of snooker on a miniature table with cue sticks in hand (Figs. 4.109 to 4.111). This scene is entitled, "Les Jeueurs des Billards" (the pool players). Another pair are found "in their cups," staggering home with bottles of wine still in their hands (Fig. 4.112). This duo has certainly earned the title of "Les Buveurs" (the drinkers).

Perhaps they are coming home from the party that was held in the next dome, which was sold by Christie's in London. Here we see a "free for all" frog fraternity party in full swing (Fig. 4.113). These boisterous amphibians are drinking, playing cards, knocking over furniture, and in general having a fun time. (A dome with a similar theme of frogs can be seen in the center window of Shaw's shop on page 106).

Another party occurs in this case from The Strong Museum (Fig. 4.114). A heated game of cards is taking place in a well-appointed parlor by four red squirrels. The room is fully detailed with floral prints gracing the walls as well as a faux marble mantle that holds a miniature dome with a clock in it. Red squirrels were common subjects as card players in anthropomorphic scenes. The Charles H. Eldon Company, taxidermists from Williamsport, Pennsylvania, in the United States, chose a humorous image of a woodpecker and a squirrel with the quote of "Who's that knocking?" on the base of the dome (Fig. 4.115).

Fig. 4.112. "Les Buveurs" (the drinkers), French, c. late 19th century.

Fig. 4.113. Frogs "Free-for-All" party, English, c. late 19th century. *Photo courtesy of Christie's, London.*

Fig. 4.114. Diorama depicting red squirrels playing cards in a parlor, English, c. late 19th century. *Photo courtesy of The Strong, Rochester, New York.*

Fig. 4.115. American taxidermist trade card, c. early 20th century.

THE CHARLES H. ELDON COMPANY
TAXIDERMISTS
331 WEST FOURTH STREET
WILLIAMSPORT, PENNA., U. S. A.
OVER THIRTY-SEVEN YEARS IN BUSINESS

Winds (Wings) of Change

During the latter part of the twentieth century taxidermy was maligned, as terms such as creepy, old-fashioned and "politically incorrect" crept into our culture. Horror movies such as Alfred Hitchcock's *Psycho* depicted the mentally deranged character of Norman Bates, whose hobby of taxidermy enabled him to stuff birds as well as his dead mother. By this time thousands of magnificent pieces were being

Fig 4.116. Mahogany ornithological cabinet by Chapell and Luce, Isle of Jersey, c. 1855.

dismantled, put into storage, or destroyed. The context in which these art works were created was forgotten or ignored. The twentieth century mentality could no longer grasp the concept of an era that viewed the natural world with an acquisitive fascination. Often referred to as specimen cabinets, this mahogany example, created in St. Helier on the Isle of Jersey in 1855 by cabinetmakers Jean Luce and J. Chapell, displays over one hundred specimens of tropical birds in its upper section. It provided ongoing entertainment and wonderment for those fortunate enough to see it (Figs. 4.116 to 4.120). Similarly, an enormous six foot

tall case housing a pair of Great Argus pheasants from Malaysia produced by James Gardner around 1870 (Figs. 4.121 to 4.123) made as much of an impression on the viewer as any big screen plasma television of today. People still stand before it in awe.

Fig. 4.119. Detail of Fig. 4.116. A laughing thrush.

Fig. 4.117. Detail of Fig. 4.116. A violet turaco.

Fig. 4.118. Detail of Fig. 4.116. A golden oriole.

Fig. 4.120. Detail of Fig. 4.116. A lesser bird of paradise with mixed species.

Fig. 4.121. Great Argus pheasants by James Gardner, c. 1870.

Fig. 4.122. Detail of Fig. 4.121.

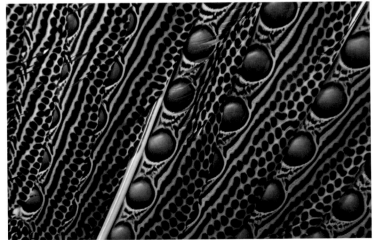

Fig. 4.123. Detail of Fig. 4.121. Ocellated pattern of the wing feathers giving this pheasant the name "Argus" after the Greek God Argus who had 100 eyes.

When viewing antique specimens of birds, whether in glass domes or cases, the frequently asked question is "Are any of these extinct?" In well over ninety-nine percent of the cases the answer is no. Presently some of the species are listed as threatened or endangered, which was not the case in the nineteenth century when they were mounted. Industrialization, deforestation, habitat loss, and human population have brought about their current status. One tragic story of extinction is that of the passenger pigeon (Fig. 4.124) whose numbers, during the early 1800s, were estimated at one billion plus. When this elegant pigeon migrated throughout the midwestern United States, it was reported that the flocks darkened the sky for days. An all-out effort began to eradicate this "nuisance" by poisoning, shooting, and burning the trees in which they were roosting. Within a one hundred-year period the passenger pigeon became extinct. The last surviving individual, Martha, died in the Cincinnati Zoo on September 1, 1914. The passenger pigeon was not a victim of the bird collector or taxidermist, it was a victim of the rapacious nature of man.

Fig. 4.124. "Gone Forever."

5

FEATHER WORK
"BIRDS OF A FEATHER"

Fig. 5.1. Feather flower bouquet illustration, *Godey's Lady's Book, photo courtesy of the Print and Picture Collection, Free Library of Philadelphia.*

With evolution, reptilian scales were replaced by feathers. It is almost as if each species of bird set about to outdo the other in the color, shape, and texture of their plumes. Whether it is the bright red feathers of a male cardinal or the resplendent display of the peacock, the ultimate goal is that of attraction. All cultures of humans have adopted this idea from the birds by choosing to adorn themselves with fine feathers. From the primitive tribes of New Guinea, (Fig. 5.2) to the infamous Victorian actress Lily Langtry (Fig. 5.3), extravagant headdresses of exotic plumes have been worn to "catch the eye."

Fig. 5.3. Lily Langtry, c. 1890.

Fig. 5.2. New Guinea wigman, *photo courtesy of Richard Demougin, Paris, France.*

The last quarter of the nineteenth century saw the heyday of these feathered fantasies that graced the female heads of western civilization. Not only was the plucked breeding plumage of exotic species found on hats, but often times the entire bird (Fig. 5.4). The millinery industry was booming and the demand for feathers soared, as hundreds of thousands of bird skins yearly were imported to London and New York. By the beginning of the twentieth century, the threat to foreign as well as indigenous species brought about the first laws to protect endangered birds both in America and abroad.

Fig. 5.4. Two "stylish" lades, c. 1890.

The art of feather work found its place in the parlor with beginnings in the eighteenth century. An advertisement in the *Boston Gazette* dated 1755 announced that:

> *Mrs. Hiller still continues to keep school in Hanover Street, where young ladies may be taught Wax-work, Transparent and Filigree, Quill-work and Featherwork...*

Bird pictures were a favorite art form during the Georgian and Victorian periods in England (Figs. 5.5 and 5.6). In 1771 Mrs. Hannah Robertson, a teacher of ornamental crafts, published *The Ladies School of Art*, where she advised on how to create pictures of "Birds executed in their own Plumage." A Mrs. Kinglon, in 1835, carried on Mrs. Robertson's work by publishing her manual, *The Wreath,* in which she discusses the methods required to create a bird picture. Every detail is covered from making the outline sketch to plucking and gluing the feathers from the model (bird) in a neat and orderly fashion.

"The eye may be one of glass and the feet and branches are to be painted by hand." (Howe, p. 133)

The following excerpt is from a poem written by William Cowper (1731-1800) in which he describes the literary salon of Mrs. Elizabeth Montagu in Portman Square, London. Mrs. Montagu was one of the founding members of The Blue Stocking Society, a group of mid-eighteenth century aristocratic women who met for lectures and discussions on art and literature.

"On Mrs. Montagu's Feather Hangings"

The birds put off their every hue
To dress a room for Montagu
The Peacock sends his heavenly dyes,
His rainbows and his starry eyes;
The Pheasant plumes, which infold
His mantling neck with downy gold;
The cock his arched tail's azure show;
And, river blanched, the Swan his snow

Figs. 5.5 & 5.6. Pair of feather work pheasant (bird) pictures, 19th century.

This feathery interior decoration was considered fashionable and nowhere else was this more evident than the drawing room at A La Ronde in Devon, England. As mentioned in chapter two, the house was built by the Misses Parminter in 1795. Over a period of years, along with the shell work decorations, this eccentric pair created a feather mosaic frieze that encircles the top of the drawing room and door surrounds (Figs. 5.7 and 5.8). Thousands of individual feathers from many species of birds comprise the repeated pattern of roundels and borders. The crowning glory is high above, where a gallery of bird portraits done in feathers is surrounded by complex designs of feathers and sea shells imbedded in every square inch of the plaster walls (Figs. 5.9 and 5.10)

Fig. 5.9. The shell and feather work gallery (bay seven) at A La Ronde, Devon. *Photo courtesy of The National Trust, U.K.*

Fig. 5.7. Feather cornice and door surround in the drawing room at A La Ronde, Devon. *Photo courtesy of The National Trust, U.K.*

Fig. 5.8. Close up view of the frieze of feathers in the drawing room at A La Ronde, Devon. *Photo courtesy of The National Trust, U.K.*

Fig. 5.10. Detail of owl feather work picture (bay seven) in the shell and feather work gallery at A La Ronde, Devon. *Photo courtesy of The National Trust, U.K.*

Some of the most exquisite examples of feather flowers under glass were made in France (Fig. 5.11). This large arrangement, although purchased in London on Portobello Road, has its origin in Paris. The flowers are crafted from a wide variety of bird species and presented in their natural state (Fig. 5.12). One can find blooms created from the downy white feathers of the swan along with the delicately formed small flowers composed of nape and breast that were plucked from a green budgie (Fig. 5.13). The patience required to make these tiny blooms daunts our modern minds.

Fig. 5.12. Detail of Fig. 5.11.

Fig. 5.13. Detail of Fig. 5.11.

Fig. 5.11. A large oval dome of natural feather flowers in a gilt wire basket, French, c. 1875.

Fig. 5.14. A pair of feather flower arrangements in Old Paris vases, French, c. 1880.

Fig. 5.15. Detail of Fig. 5.14.

Fig. 5.16. Detail of Fig. 5.14.

A matched pair of round domes, purchased in France, exhibit the use of white feathers only accented by pink satin rosebuds (Fig. 5.14). The flowers demonstrate a variety of techniques such as curled and serrated petals (Figs. 5.15 and 5.16). These wired and espaliered feathered botanical beauties are placed in appropriate Old Paris porcelain vases.

America was very interested in feather work, as evidenced by this article from *Godey's Lady's Book* in March of 1858:

The Art of Making Feather Flowers

The art of making feather flowers is scarcely known or practiced in this country; but they can be made to equal foreign productions, from the plumage of the common goose, and will, at trifling expense, produce bouquets of all the garden favorites.

The suggested materials were to include:

Good white goose or swan's feathers
A little fine wire, different sizes
A few skeins of fine floss silk
Cotton wool or wadding
A reel of No. 4 Moravian cotton
Starch and gums for paste
Pair of small sharp scissors
A few sheets of colored silk paper

When flowers other than white were desired the following watercolors or dyes could be made.

Blue – oil of vitriol to which is added indigo powder.
Yellow – A tablespoon of turmeric
Orange color – add a little bicarbonate of soda to the yellow dye
Green – Mix the indigo liquid with the turmeric
Pink – three pink pigment saucers/cakes with cream of tartar for a deep amethyst
Lilac – Two teaspoons of cudbear [a purplish-red dye derived from lichens] to which cream of tartar is added
Red – A tablespoon of prepared cochineal [a red dye made from pulverized female cochineal insects], a teaspoon of cream of tartar and a few drops of muriate of tin.

For each dye, the ingredients were put into a quart of boiling water. The cleaned feathers were then added and allowed to stay in the dye until the desired color was obtained. They were then rinsed in cool water and allowed to dry before a good fire. During the drying the feather flower artist was instructed to draw each one between the thumb and forefinger until it regained its original shape. For the artist who was not inclined to mix their own colors, commercial dyes could be purchased from firms such as Judson's.

It was also suggested that, when obtainable, the artist should procure naturally colored feathers such as the blue of the jays, the spotted feathers of guinea fowl or in the case of imitating leaves, the bright green feathers of a parrot.

Design in Feather-Work.

Fig. 5.17.

Lamp-Mat with Decoration of Feather-Flowers.

Fig. 5.18.

Fig. 5.19. Feather flower wreath in walnut shadow box, signed Anna Best 1879.

Plumes in Bloom

As with the art of wax flower making, the artist is instructed to collect two identical blooms: one from which patterns are created, and the other to serve as the model. Each feather petal was to have the lower part of its shaft glued to fine wire and then wrapped with a bit of cotton and green tissue paper. Once the flower was assembled, it could be added to a bouquet or wired into a wreath, which would be set into a deep walnut shadowbox such as this signed example created by Anna Best in 1879. It measures 37 by 33 inches (Fig. 5.19).

Fig 5.20. Detail of Fig. 5.19.

Anna used a variety of techniques, including varnishing the cut feather petals, and applying details such as spots and stripes with paint (Fig. 5.20). From 1873-1879, The Work Department in *Godey's* featured many illustrations of feather work flowers, along with those of feather butterflies (Figs. 5.21 to 5.23).

Fig. 5.21.

Fig. 5.22.

Fig. 5.23.

Fig 5.25.
Detail of Fig. 5.24.

Fig. 5.26. Detail of Fig. 5.24.

Fig. 5.24. Feather flower bouquet in cranberry glass vase, c. 1875. *From the collection of Steven and Susan Goodman.*

A dome from the Goodman collection provides protection for a bouquet of bright red and white feather flowers (Figs. 5.24 and 5.25). A wreath of white flowers covers the interior of the ebonized base. *Godey's* suggests that a perched bird would be an appropriate accent for such an arrangement, as evidenced by this petite feathered fellow whose neck and back are made from the nape feathers of a peacock (Fig. 5.26).

Hummingbirds and feather flowers are complementary companions in this English dome that contains three dozen of these avian gems (Fig. 5.27). Tiny feather flowers form a vine that wraps around the central branch of the tree (Figs. 5.28 and 5.29).

Fig. 5.29. Detail of Fig. 5.27.

Fig. 5.28. Detail of Fig. 5.27.

Fig. 5.27. A mahogany-based oval dome of three dozen hummingbirds with feather flower accents, c. 1870.

Hand screens were an essential accessory for genteel ladies during the Victorian era. They protected an ivory complexion from the heat of a roaring fire, along with producing a slight breeze when one felt overheated or faint. They could also provide a subtle blind behind which one might whisper a secret to a friend. *Ladies' Fancy Work* gave several suggestions in their chapter on feather work, such as using peacock or pheasant feathers or an entire barn owl to create a hand screen (Figs. 5.30 to 5.32). One, less cumbersome and more elegant than the barn owl example, is this hand screen made from white swan feathers (Fig. 5.33). The border is made from trimmed covert feathers of the swan's wing. The center of the screen is a nest of down feathers, accented by a spray of delicate feather flowers and leaves. The green parrot feather leaves are dotted with tiny iridescent beetles (Fig. 5.34). The scenario is complete with a hummingbird that is attracted to the simulated blooms. This was the perfect addition to one's outfit when attending a ball, the opera, or a fashionable soirée.

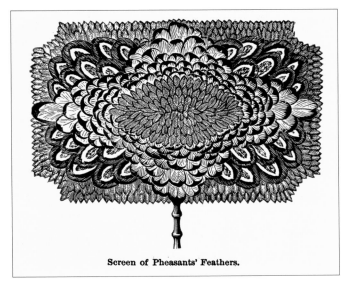

Screen of Pheasants' Feathers.

Fig. 5.31.

Screen of Peacock-Feathers.

Fig. 5.30.

Barn-Owl Hand-Screen.

Fig. 5.32.

Fig. 5.33. A hand screen made of swan feathers with feather flower decorations, c. 1880.

Fig. 5.34.
Detail of Fig. 5.33.

As mentioned in previous chapters, the cross was commonly used as an object to be decorated with nineteenth century parlor pastimes. Whether it was wax, shell, hair, wool, or, in this case, feather flowers (Fig. 5.35), this symbol of Christian morality and values found its place in many homes. In this example, white feather flowers were used exclusively to suggest purity as they entwine about the red velvet cross (Fig. 5.36).

From Picture Frame to Pill Box

Laws to protect bird species, along with changing tastes in fashion, created a decline in the use of feathers. Feathers in interior decoration experienced a brief revival in the 1970s with arrangements of peacock feathers in vases, which added an aesthetic as well as mystical touch. The days of using feathers as an art form, however, gradually dwindled and, within a one hundred year period, the feather industry has become centered on providing plumes for theatrical productions, costumes, and craft stores.

Fig 5.37.

Fig. 5.35. A velvet covered cross draped with a garland of feather flowers, c. 1875.

Fig. 5.36. Detail of Fig. 5.35.

6

BEAUTIFUL IN DEATH
"SKELETON LEAVES AND PHANTOM BOUQUETS"

Fig 6.1. "Beautiful in Death." *Photo courtesy of Michael Sage.*

They are spirits of flowers that blossomed and died
Long since in the garden- its beauty and pride;
Yet they rise from corruption, in robes new and bright,
As vision-like phantoms, all spotless and white.

Fig. 6.2. Book cover design, *Skeleton Leaves and Phantom Flowers* by J. E. Tilton, 1864.

So begins the poem published by J. E. Tilton in his 1864 book entitled, *Skeleton Leaves and Phantom Flowers: A Treatise On the Art of Producing Skeleton Leaves* (Fig. 6.2). Tilton begins his treatise by noting that the art of preparing the fibrous skeletons of leaves had its roots in China during the Ming Dynasty (1368-1644). It was then the practice to paint designs and mottoes on these lacy forms. He states that the process was first mentioned in London publications of the seventeenth century and that it was introduced into England by way of Italy during the reign of Elizabeth I.

The phantom bouquet made its American debut in 1856. It was presented as part of a display in a jewelry store window, where it created more interest than the silver and gems that surrounded it. This dismayed the shop owner, as it was the first item in the window to sell. Several more examples by the same maker sold just as quickly. The art of skeletonized leaves had arrived and America embraced it.

Throughout the 1860s,1870s, and 1880s, the popularity of these ghostly arrangements grew rapidly, with many examples being photographed and presented as the subject of stereo views (Fig. 6.3). The stereoscope was an invention that elevated photography to a new level. By placing the double-imaged card in the stereo viewer and looking through lenses the two pictures merged to create a three dimensional effect. This device provided entertainment throughout the latter half of the nineteenth century.

The attraction of skeleton leaf designs brought about an official patent regarding their preparation, granted to a Mrs. Irene L. Rogers of Springfield, Massachusetts, in 1878. Patent number 211,054 is entitled, "Improvement in the Processes of Skeletonizing Leaves" (Fig. 6.5). It states the various processes that Mrs. Rogers had created for leaves, seed vessels, and ferns that include the use of chlorate of soda, muriatic acid and chlorate of lime (bleach).

Fig. 6.3. Stereoview of phantom bouquet in dome, c. 1870. *Photo courtesy of Michael Sage.*

Fig. 6.5. Patent #211,054 for "Improvement in Processes of Skeletonizing Leaves," issued to Irene L. Rogers of Springfield, Massachusetts, on November 23, 1877. *Photo courtesy of Michael Sage.*

UNITED STATES PATENT OFFICE.

IRENE L. ROGERS, OF SPRINGFIELD, MASSACHUSETTS.

IMPROVEMENT IN PROCESSES OF SKELETONIZING LEAVES.

Specification forming part of Letters Patent No. **211,054,** dated December 17, 1878; application filed November 23, 1877.

To all whom it may concern:

Be it known that I, IRENE L. ROGERS, of Springfield, Hampden county, Commonwealth of Massachusetts, have invented new and useful Improvements in Ornamental Leaves, Flowers, Ferns, &c., for millinery and other ornamental purposes, of which the following is a specification, in which the process of manufacture is set out.

This invention relates to ornaments made from the fibrous parts of leaves, flowers, ferns, &c., after having the vegetable matter removed.

The process of manufacture is as follows: I gather the leaves or other matter at any season of the year when the fiber has become toughened. As the treatment of ferns differs somewhat from the treatment of other matter, I proceed to describe this first. I make a solution of equal parts each of chlorate of soda and rain-water, (Leaproe's chlorate of soda gives the best result,) place the ferns in a glass vessel, and cover with the above solution. Set the vessel in the sunlight, if possible, though a very good result may be had by applying artificial heat. After remaining about four hours, remove and immerse in soft water to remove the soda.

In treating leaves, flowers, seed-vessels, &c., I take from one to two gallons of rain-water and add about one tea-spoonful of muriatic acid; place the leaves, &c., in a jar loosely, and cover with the above liquid; set in a warm place (the heat of the sun is preferable) until the vegetable matter is softened and easily removed. This time varies. With the softer varieties one week is sufficient, while with others six months may be required to complete the process. I use a soft brush to remove the vegetable matter from the fiber. The fiber is then bleached in the following manner: Make a solution of one-fourth pound chlorate of lime to about eight quarts of rain-water; place the fibrous matter loosely in a glass vessel, cover with the above, and expose to the light until the fiber becomes thoroughly bleached. This usually takes about three hours. A strong sunlight gives the best result. After which the fiber should be soaked in soft water to remove the lime and foreign matter. The fibrous matter, after being colored in the ordinary way, is made into bunches or used separately for millinery or other ornamental purposes.

Having therefore described my invention, what I claim, and desire to secure by Letters Patent, is—

1. In the process of preparing leaves, flowers, seed-vessels, &c., for skeletonizing, the separation of the vegetable and fibrous material of the leaves by first softening in muriatic acid and water and subjecting to heat, and afterward removing the vegetable matter, substantially as and in the manner set forth.

2. The process of treating ferns for skeletonizing by first immersing in a solution of chloride of soda and water and subjecting to heat, then freeing the ferns from the soda by immersion in soft water, substantially as and in the manner set forth.

IRENE L. ROGERS.

Witnesses:
ALLEN WEBSTER,
LESTER NOBLE.

Fig 6.4. Arrangement of skeleton leaves on velvet in glass dome, c. 1865. *Photo courtesy of The Strong, Rochester, New York.*

The Art of Skeletonizing Leaves

Tilton suggested that to begin the process of skeletonizing the leaves, seed vessels and ferns must be gathered when they were at their peak of maturity during the month of June. Care must be taken to select only the most perfect examples that were void of blemishes and insect damage. Tilton's book went into great detail emphasizing the perfect leaf to use is one that is "sufficiently ligneous or structurally sound" (Tilton, p. 22). A variety of botanical terms were used in the treatise to define the shapes of leaves, such as serrated, acuminate (pointed), and cordate (heart-shaped). He also dedicated a section to the anatomy of a leaf, where he compared the cellular green tissue to that of the vascular tissue or veins. In the case of skeletonizing, the pattern of the veins was of great aesthetic importance. Species that were recommended include elms, maples, magnolias, poplar, sycamores, and ivy (Figs. 6.7 and 6.8).

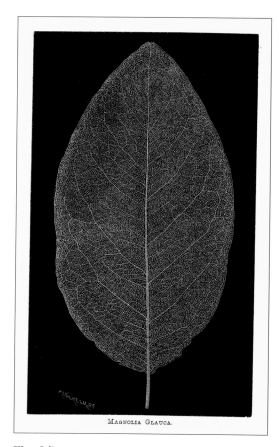

MAGNOLIA GLAUCA.

Fig. 6.7.

Fig. 6.6. Advertisement for purchasing the treatise for skeletonizing leaves.

IVY—SILVER POPLAR

Fig. 6.8.

Maceration

The verse from the Phantom Bouquet poem, "Yet they rise from corruption," best describes maceration, the next stage of the process. Here it refers to the rotting and putrefaction of the leaf's soft tissue. The gathered leaves were to be placed in an earthenware vessel and covered with rain water, then placed in a sunny spot. Mrs. Rogers, in her patent, suggested adding chlorate of sodium to accelerate the process, which may have taken two weeks to several months, depending on the species one had chosen. Patience and diligence, plus a high tolerance for foul odor, were required, as the skeletonizer must check the progress of the decomposing leaves each day.

When the green matter could be removed easily between the thumb and forefinger or with a very soft tooth brush, the process was complete. The exposed vascular structure of the leaf was now rinsed in clean water, blotted in a soft towel, and allowed to dry. It could then be pressed between sheets of white paper.

Bleaching

After completing the maceration process, the artist would begin the bleaching process. The desired effect was that of creating a ghostly white form that possessed an ethereal quality. As Edward Parrish, in his book, *"The Phantom Bouquet,"* published in 1863 (Figs. 6.9 and 6.10), states,

> *No matter how perfectly the leaves may have been skeletonized, if they are permitted to retain any shade of their original yellow, they are deficient in beauty, at least to the eye of the connoisseur.* (Parrish, p. 42)

The leaves were placed in a glass jar, stem end down, and covered with a solution of two tablespoons of bleach to each pint of water. The jar was to be covered tightly and placed in a warm sunny area. The bleaching process took six to twelve hours, with great care taken not to over bleach, as this would result in weakening the leaf's structure. After removing the leaves, they were rinsed and blotted dry once again.

Fig. 6.9. Cover design for *The Phantom Bouquet* by Edward Parrish, 1863.

THE

PHANTOM BOUQUET:

A POPULAR TREATISE ON THE ART OF

SKELETONIZING

LEAVES AND SEED-VESSELS

AND ADAPTING THEM TO

Embellish the Home of Taste.

BY

EDWARD PARRISH,

MEMBER OF THE ACADEMY OF NATURAL SCIENCES OF PHILADELPHIA, THE PHILADELPHIA COLLEGE OF PHARMACY, ETC.

PHILADELPHIA:
J. B. LIPPINCOTT & CO.
LONDON: ALFRED BENNET.
1863.

Fig. 6.10. Title page for *The Phantom Bouquet* by Edward Parrish, 1863.

Seed Vessels and Ferns

In most phantom bouquets one sees the inclusion of ferns and seed vessels. In the case of seed vessels, Mr. Parrish highly recommended those from the Stramonium (Datura) (Fig. 6.12), commonly known as devil's trumpet, and those from the Physalis or ground cherry genus. Due to their fragility, seed vessels and ferns were not subjected to the maceration process. Ferns were to be pressed and dried before bleaching. The bleaching process could take up to one week until the perfect level of whiteness was achieved (Figs. 6.13 to 6.14). After that, the whitened fronds were rinsed and pressed between sheets of white paper to dry.

Fig. 6.11. Arrangement of skeleton leaves and ferns with stramonium seed pod, c. 1865.

Fig. 6.14. Detail of Fig. 6.11.

Fig. 6.12. Skeletonized seed pod.

Fig. 6.13. Stereoview of an arrangement of skeletonized ferns and leaves under a glass dome.

Arranging the Bouquets

When the necessary components of the bouquet were processed and assembled, the skeletonizer could set about the task of creating a pleasing and tasteful arrangement. It was to be placed under a glass shade (Figs. 6.15 and 6.16) or into a shadowbox as "these will be found indispensible to the permanent preservation of what otherwise would be fleeting beauty" (Parrish, p. 39).

Fig. 6.15. Stereoview image of low arrangement of skeleton leaves shown without glass dome, c.1860. *Photo courtesy of Michael Sage.*

Fig. 6.16. A design for, "An Arrangement of Skeleton Leaves for Under a Glass Shade".

First stems were to be added to the leaves and ferns by using white silk-wrapped wire or cotton crochet thread which had been stiffened with gum arabic (Fig. 6.17). In regards to arranging the leaves, Parrish stressed the use of aesthetic sensibilities and composition by always grouping larger leaves at the bottom and smaller at the top. When using a glass dome for display it was suggested that a piece of black or dark blue velvet be used to cover the base, as this would create the proper contrast and show the leaves in a dramatic fashion, as shown in the example from the Strong Museum (Fig. 6.4). Many times the bleached seed vessel would act as the vase from which the ghostly bouquet would unfurl as found in this dome from The Wilderstein Historic Site (house museum) in Rhinebeck, New York (Fig. 6.18). The same principles of design applied to shadowboxes as well. With a circa date of 1860, this example from the Wisconsin Historical Society in Madison is a rarity (Fig. 6.19). The arrangement of leaves with a black velvet background is contained in a faux finished oval frame. The horseshoe wreath was the motif chosen for this composition of skeleton leaves and seed vessels, with bleached ferns as an accent (Figs. 6.20 to 6.22).

Fig. 6.17. A skeletonized leaf with attached silk wrapped wire, c. 1860s.

Fig. 6.18. Arrangement of skeleton leaves under glass dome with claw-footed base, circa 1860s. *From the collection of the Wilderstein Historic Site, Rhinebeck, New York.*

Fig. 6.19. Skeletonized leaves in an oval frame, c. 1860s, donated by Susanna Parr (born c. 1882) who was a public school teacher in Milwaukee. *Photo courtesy of Wisconsin Historical Society, image 55204.*

Fig. 6.21. Detail of Fig. 6.20.

Fig. 6.22. Detail of Fig. 6.20.

Fig. 6.20. Arrangement of skeletonized leaves, ferns, and seed pods in a horseshoe shape displayed in a walnut shadow box, c. 1875.

Some other ideas were to use a velvet-covered cross (Figs. 6.23 to 6.25) as a form or to take a shadow box and create a tilt-top top table that would serve both as a decorative and functional object in the parlor.

In each case Edward Parrish stressed the concept of aesthetics and informed the reader that the phantom bouquet would prove to be a "perennial source of enjoyment" by stating that: "In summer, its fleecy whiteness recalls the hoar-frost and snow-flakes so pleasantly associated with the season of active exercise and cold and bracing air." And in contrast, "On dreary winter days the bouquet may serve to recall many a happy hour spent among the trees clad in their summer verdure" (Parrish p. 42).

Parrish concluded his treatise with a statement that exemplifies Victorian romanticism by writing:

Nor is this fair ornament destitute of the highest function of nature and art—to lift the soul from grovelling things up to the regions of poetry and love. (Parrish p. 43)

An Ivy-Leaf Cross. Design in Skeleton Leaves.

Fig. 6.24. Design for a cross made of skeletonized ivy leaves from *Household Elegancies*, 1877.

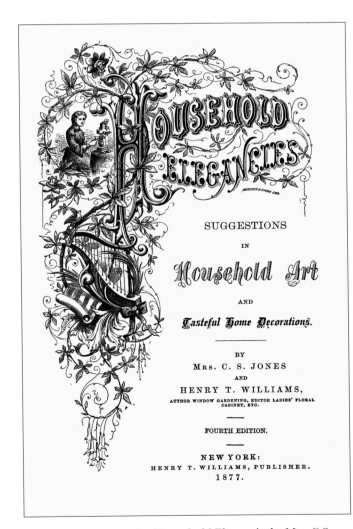

Fig. 6.23. Title page for *Household Elegancies* by Mrs. C.S. Jones & Henry T. Williams, 1877.

Fig. 6.25. Stereoview of skeletonized leaves in the shape of a cross, c. 1870s. *Photo courtesy of Michael Sage.*

Beautiful in Death: Phantom Bouquets as Memorials

The use of skeleton leaves and phantom bouquets was widespread in memorializing the dead. As discussed in the previous chapter on hair work, in modern times the practice of mourning reached a high point during the nineteenth century. The phantom bouquet became an obvious choice when representing and remembering the departed. William C. Darrah, in his book *The World of Stereographs*, devotes a small section to skeleton leaf arrangements. He

Fig. 6.26. The Martyrs-Lincoln & Garfield, copyright 1884, by Littleton View Co. *Photo courtesy of Michael Sage.*

Fig. 6.27. Skeleton Leaves, Charles Sumner memorial, John B. Soule, 199 Washington St., Boston. *Photo courtesy of Michael Sage.*

Fig. 6.28. Stereoview of phantom bouquet as memorial to Henry Ward Beecher. *Photo courtesy of Michael Sage.*

makes reference to the before-mentioned Mrs. Irene Rogers who, along with registering a patent for her process of skeletonizing, also copyrighted about thirty of her arrangements which were stereographed by John P. Soule (1828-1904) of Boston.

A large majority of these stereoviews depicted cabinet cards of deceased presidents, such as Abraham Lincoln (1809-1865) and James Garfield (1831-1881) (Fig. 6.26), as well as noted abolishionists Senator Charles Sumner (1811-1874) (Fig. 6.27) and Henry Ward Beecher (1813-1887) (Fig. 6.28). Eventually photographer Benjamin W. Kilburn obtained the rights to Mrs. Rogers's images and continued to reproduce them until 1895. The firm of Edward and Henry T. Anthony of New York was one of the largest suppliers of photographic materials and produced many stereoviews of phantom bouquets (Fig. 6.29). Throughout the last quarter of the nineteenth century one finds an abundance of funeral skeleton leaf arrangements, depicting wreaths with a portrait of the deceased, in the trade lists of American photographers. As the dawning of the twentieth century took place, stereo viewers, as well the art of the phantom bouquet, became merely ghosts of the past.

Fig. 6.31. Phantom Leaves, Abraham Lincoln memorial. *Photo courtesy of Michael Sage.*

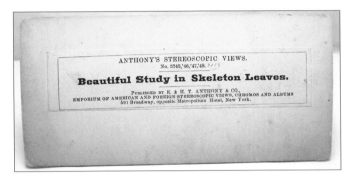

Fig. 6.29. Beautiful Study in Skeleton Leaves, Anthony's Stereoscopic Views (reverse of stereo card) by E. & H. T. Anthony & Co. *Photo courtesy of Michael Sage.*

Fig. 6.30. Phantom bouquet memorial, Abraham Lincoln, Died April 15, 1865. *Photo courtesy of Michael Sage.*

Fig. 6.33. "A Thing of Beauty is a Joy for Ever." *Photo courtesy of Michael Sage.*

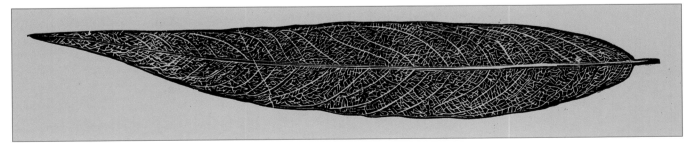

Fig. 6.32. A skeletonized willow leaf.

7
WOOL WORK
"HAVE YOU ANY WOOL?"

Fig. 7.1. Wool flower dome. *From the Leo Lerman/Gray Foy Collection.*

Berlin Work

One of the revered attributes of a nineteenth century lady was her skilled needlework. Whether it was knitting, crocheting, embroidery, or needlepoint every refined young lady was encouraged to use a needle in a practical and artistic manner. Every month *Godey's Lady's Book* published articles on different techniques and suggested projects relating to the art of fine handwork. One of the most popular forms of needlepoint was Berlin wool work. During the early part of the nineteenth century a skilled German embroiderer, Madame Wittich, created patterns on sheets of squared paper that could readily be transferred onto canvas. The patterns were generally robust floral designs such as the one pictured here (Fig. 7.2). Other subjects, such as dogs and cats on plump cushions, bucolic scenes, and religious icons, were common. Entire kits could be purchased that included brightly colored wool (also from Germany) and instructions for creating stitches such as the German Diamond, the Victoria pattern, the Algerine, and the Velvet (Howe, p.154). The combination of these techniques produced a lush three-dimensional effect not seen before in needlework. This "stitch by number" approach revolutionized needlework and made it easier for the less artistic to create beautiful, worked panels that could be applied to chair seats, footstools, and fire screens. In many cases, beadwork was included in the design.

An article from the February 1853 issue of *Godey's* is entitled, "Instructions for Making Miss Lambert's Registered Crochet Flowers." It begins:

Miss Lambert, having seen the very beautiful vase of flowers, worked in Berlin wool, that obtained the honorable mention in the Great Exhibition, was struck with its simplicity and beauty; and being convinced that, were it generally known, would become universally popular, she purchased the idea of the inventor, and now begs to lay it before the public.

Miss Lambert goes on to point out the convenience of making crochet flowers as opposed to those made in wax or from shells:

In its occupation ladies can spend their leisure hours delightfully in the garden, the drawing-room, or the seaside, as neither tints nor gum are required, but merely the wool and the crochet-hook.

Fig. 7.2. A panel of Berlin (wool) and bead work flowers, c.1865.

The Art of Making Wool Flowers

The article, which is profusely illustrated (Fig. 7.3 to 7.7), takes the reader through the step-by-step creation of a variety of crocheted leaves under the heading of "To Form the Leaf." After creating the suggested leaves, one could advance to the next heading of "To Make the Flowers." This category consisted of three subdivisions or classes: "Class I- Petalled Flowers;" "Class II- For Making the Lily;" and "Class III- To make Bell Flowers." Miss Lambert specifies that the only materials required are "Berlin wool of the best quality, which may be had of all colors, a small quantity of the finest iron wire, and the common crochet hook."

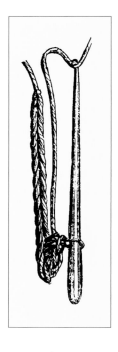

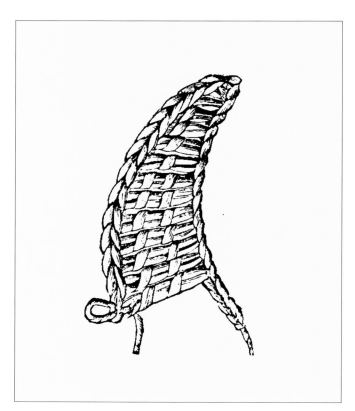

Figs. 7.3 to 7.7. Illustrations from *Godey's Lady's Book*, 1853. *Photos courtesy of the Print and Picture Collection, Free Library of Philadelphia.*

Under Miss Lambert's tutelage the needle worker could try her hand at recreating garden favorites such as roses, dahlias, pansies, poppies, and the more challenging camellia. The illustrations in *Godey's,* along with the detailed stitch-by-stitch directions show the reader how to create a simple leaf, a geranium leaf, and a round petal using four principal crochet stitches: the chain (or foundation); the plain; the double stitch; and the long or open stitch. After completing each leaf or petal the thin wire is inserted along the perimeter, with the remaining length of wire forming a stem, which is wrapped in wool as well. A review of these detailed instructions and techniques makes it obvious that they were not for the novice. The culmination of these instructions could be a crocheted flower vase mat, as suggested in *Godey's,* or an arrangement of woolen blooms under a glass dome similar to the one from the Goodman collection (Fig. 7.8 to 7.10).

Fig. 7.8. A large oval based dome filled with brilliant wool-work flowers, c. 1860. *From the Steven and Susan Goodman Collection.*

Fig. 7.9. Detail of Fig. 7.8.

Fig. 7.10. Detail of Fig. 7.8.

Prior to Miss Lambert's published instructions, *Godey's Lady's Book* devoted six months of articles, from January through June, 1851, and April through December, 1852, on how to create knitted flowers, berries, and fruit. The 1851 articles went into detail about how to use basic knitting and purling stitches to make "marygolds, sweet peas, tulips, periwinkles and roses." The needle worker assumed the role of an amateur botanist as she read how to form stamens, pistils, calyxes, and tendrils, all rendered in colored wool. The 1852 series of articles dealt with how to make knitted berries and fruit such as "holly and its berries, mistletoe and its berries, acorn and oak leaves, a pear, and strawberries" (Fig. 7.11). Details such as spots, stripes, and seeds were to be embroidered onto the petals or berries to achieve the desired effect.

Fig. 7.11. A group of crocheted wool strawberries.

Another example of using fine wire as a superstructure is seen in this entry of 1864, "The Convolvulus, Made On Wire" (Fig. 7.12). The funnel-shaped flower was made from nine matching loops of wire, gathered together to form a frame on which the wool was alternately woven. *Godey's* suggested using white wool for the inner two-thirds of the bloom and finishing with yellow wool for the remainder.

A variety of very fine wires were manufactured for use in all of this handiwork. One type of wire found in wool (and woven silk) flower arrangements is coiled wire. This spring-like, 30-32 gauge wire was used to form a myriad of petal shapes ranging from the lily to the forget-me-not. The wool flower artist, using one, two or three-ply wool, starts at the base of the petal and stretches the fiber across the form in a radiating pattern to fill the void (Fig. 7.13). In this large 25 inch high round dome, a cross covered in roses uses this technique extensively. The ambitious artist did not neglect the reverse side of the cross either (Fig. 7.14). Flanking the cross are white lilies and a bouquet of roses. The green leaves of the lilies readily illustrate the use of the coiled wire (Fig. 7.15).

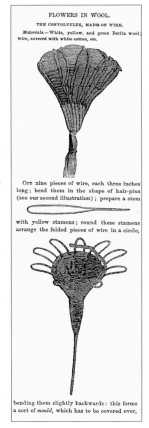

Fig. 7.12. Illustration from *Godey's Lady's Book*, 1864. *Photo courtesy of the Print and Picture Collection, Free Library of Philadelphia.*

Fig. 7.14. Wool-on-wire flower cross, reverse side of Fig. 7.13.

Fig. 7.13. A large wool-on-wire flower cross with accent bouquets, c. 1870.

Fig. 7.15. Detail of Fig. 7.13.

Coiled wire is used exclusively in this 20 inch high dome that contains a decorative basket holding an arrangement of wool flowers (Fig. 7.16). An abundance of multicolored flowers fill the basket along with decorating the handle (Fig. 7.17). A wreath of wool flowers encircles the base of the basket, which would support the Victorian attitude that no space should remain unadorned. Mother Nature is represented in the dried grasses accenting the basket and the butterfly hoping to find nectar in the wooly blooms (Fig. 7.18).

After mastering all the techniques, the wool artist might exhibit her versatility by making botanical bouquets where crocheted, knitted, and coiled wire flowers are combined (Fig. 7.19 to 7.22). Artistic license was taken by representing moss in blue crocheted yarn (Fig. 7.23). A small "beginner-size" round dome holds a nosegay of wool flowers held in a petite Chinese export vase (Fig. 7.24). It was purchased on eBay from the United Kingdom and although not the most extraordinary example, it does have its original label on the underside of its base telling us that "Davis & Co. Glass Shade Merchants of 33, Union Street, Bristol [made] Glass Shades of Superior Brilliancy" (Fig. 7.25).

Fig. 7.16. A wicker basket of wool-on-wire flowers with natural grasses and a monarch butterfly, c. 1865.

Fig. 7.17. Detail of Fig. 7.16.

Fig. 7.18. Detail of Fig. 7.16.

Fig. 7.19. A bouquet of wool work flowers exhibiting a variety of techniques, c. 1870.

Figs. 7.20 to 7.23. Details of Fig. 7.19.

Fig. 7.24. A small dome of wool-work flowers in a Chinese export porcelain vase. The dome's base has a label from Davis & Co. Glass Shade Merchants, 33 Union Street, Bristol (England).

Fig. 7.25. Label from dome in Fig. 7.24.

Another tall and narrow oval dome, purchased in Bucks County, Pennsylvania, has an added attraction of a gesso and gilt base done in an egg and dart pattern (Fig. 7.26 and 7.27). The primitive and stylized character of the flowers found in all of these examples exemplifies the folk art quality of this parlor pastime. The Brooklyn Museum in New York displays this formal pair of wool flower bouquets under glass on the mantle in the Colonel Robert J. Milligan parlor from Saratoga Springs, New York, c. 1854-56 (Fig. 7.28 and 7.29). The Rococo Revival Parlor or drawing room, along with the Gothic Revival Library, was offered to the museum intact in 1940. All architectural elements and the original furnishings were purchased by the museum for $3,000.00. Included in the sale were the original paid receipts for most of the furnishings including the parlor suite, gilt mirror, white marble mantle and ingrain carpet. These documents provide an accurate reference to the cost(s) of such luxury items during the mid-nineteenth century. The wool flowers exhibit a look of naturalism that was popular during that period.

Fig. 7.26. Large narrow oval dome of wool flowers with a gilt egg and dart decorated base, c. 1875.

Fig. 7.27.
Detail of Fig. 7.26.

Fig. 7.28. Naturalistic wool flower arrangement in an Old Paris vase in a square rosewood-based dome from the Robert J. Milligan Parlor, c. 1855. *Photo courtesy of The Brooklyn Museum.*

Fig. 7.29. Mate to Fig. 7.28 from the Robert J. Milligan Parlor, c. 1855. *Photo courtesy of The Brooklyn Museum.*

Wool Aviaries Under Glass

Flowers were not the only subject used by the needle worker. Birds and small mammals were also captured in wool and arranged on branches under domes (Fig. 7.30). This charming oval dome was purchased at the on-site sale of a Louisiana plantation. The inhabitants were created using mohair wool and detailed with beaded eyes and wire feet. The setting includes a papier-mâché tree with a mirror pond at its base, on which a wool swan is swimming. A chipmunk and a rabbit nestled in the hollow of the tree join the birds as well as an embroidered butterfly (Figs. 7.31 and 7.32).

Fig. 7.30. A moss-covered tree displaying mohair wool-work birds, a squirrel, a rabbit, and butterflies, purchased from an estate sale in Louisiana, c. 1865.

Fig. 7.31. Detail of Fig. 7.30.

Fig. 7.32. Detail of Fig. 7.30.

An outstanding example of wool birds is on display at the Metropolitan Museum of Art in New York City (Fig. 7.33). It can be found in the Richard and Gloria Manney Rococo Revival Parlor in the American Wing. This thirty-inch high round dome contains a complete aviary that revolves around a central dowel. The birds in this example achieve a realistic appearance with a variety of worked details that identify certain species. It is a perfect accent in this period room that features ornately carved rosewood furniture by John Henry Belter.

An oval-based dome in the Strong Museum collection houses a grouping of birds done in plush wool work (Fig. 7.34). The ten birds are perched on a wire tree covered in green wool. Surrounding the base of the tree is a mound of intensely colored wool pansies, lilies, and fuchsias that complete this cheerful arrangement (Fig. 7.35).

Thoroughly Modern Women

As the twentieth century progressed and more women entered the work force, needlework no longer helped define a woman's place in society. A woman was now being judged by her performance in the workplace rather than how "neatly" her stitches were executed on a fire screen or tea cosy. Providing for her family took precedent over the genteel parlor art of wool work. During the 1970s, a brief revival occurred in the fiber arts. Quilting, latch hook rug making, macramé, and needlepoint experienced a rebirth. Former American football star Roosevelt (Rosey) Greir "came out" as an avid needle worker when he authored *Rosey Grier's Needlepoint For Men* in 1973. Touting that doing needlepoint would help relieve stress and aid in the relaxation from the daily trials and tribulations that men encounter, Rosey proved by example that such hobbies were not for women alone.

Fig. 7.33. A large gilt-based round dome containing an aviary of "realistic" plush wool-work birds perched in a moss-covered tree, located in the Richard and Gloria Manney Rococo Revival Parlor, c. 1855. *Photo courtesy of The Metropolitan Museum of Art, New York.*

Fig. 7.35. Detail of Fig. 7.34.

Fig. 7.34. A folky arrangement of brightly colored plush wool work birds perched on a wool-work tree that sprouts from a mound of wool flowers, c. 1865. *Photo courtesy of The Strong, Rochester, New York.*

8
GLASS WHIMSIES
"CONFECTIONS IN GLASS"

Fig. 8.1. Boy and girl posed with glass (lamp work) ship and cross in a dome, c. late 19th century.

It has been suggested that there was more glass produced during the nineteenth century than at any time prior or since. Glass, once thought a miraculous substance that goes through the metamorphosis of solid to liquid to solid, has intrigued man's imagination since its creation in ancient times. With basic ingredients of silica (sand), soda ash, and lime, glass has served a multitude of purposes both utilitarian and decorative. One such decorative technique is called "lampwork." Lampworking or flameworking was first practiced by the Syrians in the first century B.C. It reached its height during the 14th century in Murano, Italy, where fanciful goblets, plates, and vases were made with applied lampwork creatures such as birds, seahorses, and flowers, similar to this 19th century piece from The Strong Museum (Fig. 8.2).

The materials required for lampworking were quite rudimentary, including an oil lamp, metal tweezers, and a variety of colored glass rods or canes. The glass preferred was called soda-lime, which tends to be softer and therefore more malleable when heated. The glass artist would blow air through a tube into the flame as he heated the glass rod, which served as the base for a flower or animal. He would then turn the rod, pulling its molten section and using twisting motions along with the force of gravity, to create the desired shape. Additional forms would be made in various colors in the similar way and then applied to the base shape to suggest legs, leaves, or fins. Thus an entire glass menagerie could be created, as seen in this whimsically charming dome from the collection of Steven and Susan Goodman (Fig. 8.3). Standing on an intricately worked glass platform, a long-legged blown glass bird stands guard over its nest of eggs appearing to ward off a swarm of glass butterflies. Beneath this scene a procession of glass whimsies, including a pair of swans pulling a glass chariot containing glass cat-o-nine-tails as passengers encircle the base. A miniature lighthouse adds even more novelty to an already delightful arrangement (Fig. 8.4). From the same collection, a diminutive dome covers a three-tiered compote of tiny glass fruit with a green glass bird perched on top (Fig. 8.5).

During the nineteenth century fairs and charity bazaars were popular forms of entertainment. Glass blowers and lampworkers traveled from town to town creating a variety of glass novelties.

> The glass-blowers made a goodly array and gave away tokens as they went. The men wore caps and hats brittle with wavy plumes of spun glass whilst birds, ships, goblets and decanters on their poles glistened in the beams of the hot sun.
> Mrs. Linnaeus Banks
> (Coronation Day 19 July 1821)
> *The Manchester Man* (Howe, pg.194)

Another account comes from a young English girl, Emily Shore, in her journal dated 1831, when she

Fig. 8.2. Lamp work ornament of a glass bird on an ornate glass stand, c. 1880. *Photo courtesy of The Strong, Rochester, New York.*

visited a fair and was mesmerized by the skill of the traveling glassblower:

> He made glass baskets, candle-sticks, birds, and horses. And the way he did them is as follows. He sat at a little table and before him was a little furnace which contained a flame of intense heat though it was only kept by tallow.
> He had a great many glass sticks of various sizes and every colour; when he wished to make anything- a basket for instance- he took a small one he used merely as a prop; he held one end of another in the flame till the end of it melted into a sort of paste which could be drawn out into any fineness. By this way, he made a vast number of things. One was Charles II under the Oak; another was the Lord Mayor's coach; and George IV lying in state. Some of these things were handsome and expensive. We bought a few of the minor things. One was a glass pen and an elegant and beautiful ship.
> *The Journal of a Young Naturalist*
> (1891) (Howe, pg. 194)

Fig. 8.4. Detail of Fig. 8.3.

Fig. 8.3. Fanciful lamp work arrangement in dome, c. 1870. *From the Steven and Susan Goodman Collection.*

Fig. 8.5. Lamp work miniature compote with bird, c.1880. *From the Steven and Susan Goodman Collection.*

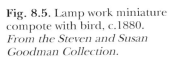

Confections in Glass

These ornaments were commonly known as "friggers." The word frigger is derived from the verb friggle or to fuss. It also refers to glass objects that serve no utilitarian purpose. The beautiful glass ship Emily purchased that day was a popular novelty commonly found under glass domes, with every detail from the miniature sailors climbing the spider web-like rigging to the tiny flags atop the masts (Fig. 8.6). The City Art Gallery in Bristol, England, has an interesting 19th century article published by a Mr. Davis and his partner Mr. Johnson that announces:

To assure the public that they are the only glass ship-builders travelling the Kingdom and that they (also) will blow any article wanted while the company are present. Glass Blowing, Spinning, Linking and Modelling.

(Howe, p.198)

Fig. 8.6. Lamp work ships with sailors, c. 1885. *Photo courtesy of David Klutho.*

Fig. 8.7. Large lamp work arrangement with ships, lighthouse, reindeer, and chariot, c. 1880.

Small fleets of glass ships floating on a sea of chipped and spun glass were displayed under glass with an accompanying glass lighthouse, as seen in this large dome (Figs. 8.7 and 8.8). The dome also includes a glass chariot holding a frozen Charlotte figure being pulled by blown glass deer on a higher tier. A similar example from the Strong Museum includes a white glass anchor in a bed of flowers, which is the symbol of hope (Fig. 8.9). In general, there is no rhyme or reason for the subjects depicted in lampwork domes. They epitomize the concept of whimsy as it was so near and dear to the Victorian heart.

Fig. 8.8. Detail of Fig. 8.7.

Fig. 8.9. Lamp work arrangement of glass novelties including ships, lighthouse, birds and anchor, c. 1875. *Photo courtesy of The Strong, Rochester, New York.*

A specific nautical story is captured under this dome from the Leo Lerman/Gray Foy collection (Fig. 8.10). This piece pays tribute to an American clipper ship *The Pampero*, presumably named for the strong winds that blow across Brazil and Argentina in the southern hemisphere. The photo card that accompanied the dome has the inscription:

My Uncle Capt. Calvin Coggins sailed the Pampero around the world in the year 1853 by the way of Cape Horn and San Francisco. It took nine months to make the trip. Capt. Coggins was born in Lubec, Me, 1825-1902, Joseph A. De Laittier, 2100 No. 2nd St. Minneapolis, Minn. (Fig. 8.11)

The *Pampero* was built in 1853 in Mystic, Connecticut, by Charles Mallory. It weighed 1375 tons and measured 202 by 38 by 21 feet. It was owned by J. Bishop & Co. of New York, and eventually provided government transport during the Civil War, before being sold in 1867. With lookouts on the crocheted glass lighthouse and an escort of smaller glass ships, this dome commemorates the return of the *Pampero* to its home port.

Fig. 8.11. Detail of Fig. 8.10.

Fig. 8.10. Lamp work figures under dome commemorating "The *Pampero*," c. 1850s. *From the Leo Lerman/ Gray Foy Collection.*

Another dome from the Lerman/ Foy collection houses a pair of flamboyant birds with plumes made of spun glass (Fig. 8.12). This piece was purchased in England and hand-carried on the plane back to New York by Mr. Foy many years ago. A similar example suggests a carousel of glass whimsies featuring a candelabra, a fountain, a birdbath with doves, a stork, and a scale (Fig. 8.13). Two elegant birds of paradise are perched high above on their nest, while beneath them a glass cupid draws back his bow (Fig. 8.14 and 8.15).

Fig. 8.12. Pair of lamp work and spun glass birds on a crocheted glass pedestal, c. 1860. *From the Leo Lerman/ Gray Foy Collection.*

Fig. 8.14. Detail of Fig. 8.13.

Fig. 8.15. Detail of Fig. 8.13.

Fig. 8.13. Magnificent arrangement of lamp work whimsies including birds, a ship, a fountain, a balance scale, a candelabra, and a cupid, c. 1880.

Smaller compositions of blown glass birds with tails made from spun glass, arranged in a tiered "Follies" configuration, were favorite subjects under shades (Fig. 8.16 to 8.19).

Simplicity in design may be found in this low round dome from the Strong Museum that houses a pair of blown glass swans with flower wreaths on their necks, courting one another on a painted pond (Fig. 8.20). The artist has cleverly suggested plants by painting them on the inner perimeter of the dome.

Fig. 8.17. Detail of Fig. 8.16.

Fig. 8.16. Three plump lamp work and spun glass birds with lamp work flowers, c. 1885.

Fig. 8.19. Detail of Fig. 8.18.

Fig. 8.18. Arrangement of three lamp work and spun glass birds with flowers, c. 1885.

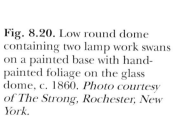

Fig. 8.20. Low round dome containing two lamp work swans on a painted base with hand-painted foliage on the glass dome, c. 1860. *Photo courtesy of The Strong, Rochester, New York.*

Fig. 8.21. Incredible bouquet of lamp work flowers in a crocheted glass basket, c.1860. *From the Steven and Susan Goodman Collection.*

Fig. 8.22. Detail of Fig. 8.21.

Glass Flowers

A rare example from the Goodman collection is a beautiful bouquet of lamp work flowers arranged in a fanciful crocheted red glass basket (Fig. 8.21). An articulated glass chain encircles the rim of the basket. The virtuosity of the lamp work flowers is remarkable, with no two blooms being alike (Fig. 8.22).

One cannot discuss nineteenth century lamp work flowers and not mention the Glass Flowers at the Harvard Museum of Natural History in Cambridge, Massachusetts. The story of these incredible glass sculptures is as fascinating as the flowers themselves. Formally known as The Ware Collection of Blaschka Glass Models of Plants, these glass specimens are in a class all their own. The father and son team of Leopold (1822-1895) and Rudolf Blaschka (1857-1939) created more than 3,000 models during the period of 1887 to 1936 at

their studio in Hosterwitz, Germany, near Dresden. Dresden was a center for glass manufacturing, so it was only natural that Leopold, possessing artistic talent, joined the family business, which produced glass ornaments and glass eyes. In the late 1850s, soon after Rudolf was born, Leopold began creating glass models of exotic flowers that he saw pictured in books. A local royal, Prince Camille de Rohan, heard about his work and commissioned 100 glass models of orchids from his private collection. Leopold also had a fascination with marine invertebrates and, using his own advanced techniques, created them in glass. His reputation as a glass model maker spread quickly and, in 1880, he was contracted by the Boston Society of Natural History Museum to create over 130 glass models of sea slugs, jellyfish, and other invertebrates. Rudolf joined his father in this project and eventually became an expert in lamp work and the glass painter for all future works.

Fig. 8.23. Bouquet of lamp work flowers "dedicated to Mrs. and Miss Ware by R. Blaschka." *Photo courtesy of Archives of Rudolph and Leopold Blaschka and The Ware Collection of Blaschka Glass Models, Harvard University, Cambridge, Massachusetts, USA.*

In 1886, after seeing the glass invertebrates in Boston and learning of the Blaschkas' talents, George Goodale, who was in the process of establishing the Harvard Botanical Museum, travelled to Dresden to make a proposal to Leopold and Rudolf. That proposal was to create a series of botanical specimens in glass as teaching aids for the school and museum. Reluctantly the Blaschkas agreed, and they set about making the first models. Those first models did not fare well during shipment to America, but there was enough left intact to pique the interest of one of Goodale's former students, Mary Lee Ware, and her mother Elizabeth Ware. The Wares financed the project, which spanned the next fifty years. Rudolf was responsible for the production after his father's death in 1895, and as a token of his appreciation created this exquisite bouquet of glass flowers bound together by a glass ribbon with the inscription, "Dedicated to Mrs. & Miss Ware, R. Blaschka" (Fig. 8.23). Of the 3000 models created by the Blaschkas, 847 species are represented, not only as scientific models but also as full artistic studies, such as the meadow lily, *Lilium canadense* (Fig. 8.24) and the fragrant water lily, *Nymphea odorata* (Fig. 8.25). The glass flowers have recently undergone extensive restoration that required elaborate measures and painstaking effort due to their extremely fragile nature. They are no longer looked upon as scientific models only, but are revered as true works of art.

Fig. 8.24. Meadow Lily, *Lilium canadense. Photo courtesy of Archives of Rudolph and Leopold Blaschka and The Ware Collection of Glass Models, Harvard University, Cambridge, Massachusetts, USA.*

Fig. 8.25. Fragrant Water Lily, *Nymphea odorata. Photo courtesy of Archives of Rudolph and Leopold Blaschka and The Ware Collection of Glass Models, Harvard University, Cambridge, Massachusetts, USA.*

The Flame Still Burns

The tradition of lamp worked glass continues in Murano, Italy, where classical forms and motifs are incorporated into contemporary design. A world of modern glass artists exists, with their work being exhibited at upscale craft shows and in major museums throughout the world. The tallow lamp of the nineteenth century has long been replaced by the intense flame of butane and acetylene torches. Glass figurines and novelties may still be purchased in gift shops worldwide, but they can never surpass the glass whimsies under domes of the nineteenth century that amazed and delighted people of all ages, and still do.

9
FANCY THAT!
"PAPER, MUSLIN SILK, BEAD, AND SEED WORK"

Fig. 9.1. Gosse-Perier Exhibit of artificial flowers from the Centennial Exhibition of 1876.
Photo courtesy of the Print and Picture Collection, Free Library of Philadelphia.

Fig. 9.2. *Mary Delany (née Granville),* by John Opie, oil on canvas, 1782. *NPG-1030, National Portrait Gallery, London.*

Paper Making

Materials such as acrylic, polyester, silicone, and polyurethane did not exist prior to the twentieth century. Celluloid was invented in the nineteenth century by an Englishman, Alexander Parkes, but it found its uses in things such as men's collars, writing pens, and eventually photographic film. Parlor pastimes that simulated the beauty of nature relied solely on natural materials. One of the simplest was paper.

Papermaking dates back to 2nd century China during the Han Dynasty, when Cai Lun, an official of the Imperial Court, combined fibers of mulberry, old rags, and hemp waste in water, which created a slurry. This slurry was then poured evenly onto a wooden framed screen called a "deckle" and allowed to drain. While damp, these fibers were turned out onto a felt sheet, and the process was repeated until a stack was produced (layers of paper and felt are called a "post"). The post was then heavily weighted to remove the remaining water, producing sheets of paper that would be hung to dry.

After being introduced to western civilization, the concept of creating paper from fibers caught on immediately. Hand-made papers have continued to be made throughout the centuries and they are valued in relation to their "rag content." Most modern day papers such as newsprint, wrapping paper, towel paper, etc., are derived from wood pulp. The process of creating paper from wood pulp was developed in 1844 by a Canadian inventor, Charles Fenerty. This put an end to the 2000-year-old process of creating paper commercially from pulped rags and started the decimation of the great forests of the world.

The first use of paper in Europe in a decorative, three-dimensional art form occurred during the Renaissance. French and Italian monks practiced the art of "quilling," which involves taking strips of paper and wrapping them around a quill to form a coil. After gluing them at their tips, these shaped coils would be arranged to create leaves, flowers, and scenes. This technique was used to decorate book covers and religious items, and eventually became popular with upper class ladies during the eighteenth century. One renowned lady of eighteenth century England was Mary Delany (nee Granville) (1700-1788) (Fig. 9.2). With her patrician background and the reputation of being an artist and society gossip, she spent her life surrounded by the aristocracy and the social elite. Mary's life was a fascinating one, attending private concerts by the composer George Frideric Handel and receiving art lessons from William Hogarth. She counted among her friends Alexander Pope, Jonathan Swift, as well as her benefactors, the Duchess of Portland (mentioned in Chapter 2), King George III, and Queen Charlotte.

At age 72, four years after her second husband's death, Mrs. Delany began an artistic endeavor for which she would become famous. She created what she referred to as her "Paper Mosaicks" (Figs. 9.3 and 9.4). These are nearly 1000 botanical studies made from layers of paper that she colored herself with pigments ground by mortar and pestle. From each sheet of hand-tinted paper she extracted petals, sepals, pistils, stamens, and stems, which were glued onto black paper, creating a stunningly dramatic effect. With scissors and scalpel sharp knives, she meticulously cut out four or five hues of red and orange to create the subtle folds in the petal of a poppy or over one hundred frilled pieces of purple and pink to replicate the delicate filaments surrounding the stigmas and anthers of the passionflower. Mrs. Delany's *Catalogue of Plants Copyed From Nature in Paper Mosaick,* finished in the year 1778, was not only an artistic tour de force, but an accurate reference for botanical research for over one hundred years after her death. This incredible collection of paper flower collages can be found in The British Museum in London.

Fig. 9.3. *Crinum Zeylanicum,* Asphodil lily, a paper collage, Mary Delany. © *The Trustees of the British Museum.*

Fig. 9.4. *Bombax Celba,* a paper collage, Mary Delany. © *The Trustees of the British Museum.*

Fig. 9.5.

The Art of Paper Flower Making

The nineteenth century witnessed an increasing interest in paper flowers, particularly those done in three dimensions. In the back of their 1840s treatise, *Lessons in Flower & Fruit Modelling in Wax,* the Mintorn brothers (mentioned in chapter one) also supplied materials for making paper flowers (Figs. 9.6 and 9.7). *Godey's Ladys' Book* advised their readers on the pleasures of creating flowers from paper in a series of articles from April to December in 1858 by stating, "Among the many agreeable occupations of ladies, the making of paper flowers deserves the first place."

Godey's recommended two basic tools: a pair of nippers (tweezers) five inches long, and a ball (ended) tool for molding the center of each petal into a hollow form. It was also suggested that the appropriate colored papers and pre-made "flower parts such as the hearts [stamens and pistils covered by a calyx], buds, leaves, etc. can be obtained at the fancy stores." For the remaining months, *Godey's* published illustrations of patterns to create such favorite blooms as the rose, the carnation, the daisy and the field poppy. Three basic steps were used: the cutting out of the petals in the appropriate colors of paper; the "goffering" or shaping and frilling of the petals; and the construction of the flower. Similar techniques to those used in the art of wax flower making were recommended by *Godey's.*

List of Prices, &c.

	s. d.		s. d.
Scissors	1 6	Wires . 3d. to	0 6
Moulders	0 6	Gum Water .	0 6
Pincers 6d. and	1 3	Silk . . .	0 6

Leaves.

	s. d.		s. d.
Rose	0 6	Orange .	0 4
to 2s. 6d. per doz.		Fuchsia .	0 4
Jasmine	0 5	Rhododendron	0 6
Camellia	0 6	Nemophila .	0 4
May	0 4	Pyrus . .	0 4
Geranium	0 6		

Others in proportion.

Hearts . . . from 2d. to 1s. per doz.
Buds . . . „ 2d. to 1s. „
Calyx Rose . „ 6d. „

A large variety of Buds, Calyx, Hearts, &c.

LIST OF PRICES

Of Materials, &c., for Paper Flowers, Imported and Manufactured

By J. H. MINTORN.

French Papers per Sheet.

Carmine	4d.
Pinks from	1d. to 3d.
Cherry	4d.
Shaded for Roses	1½d.
Or by the doz. assorted . . .	1s.
Stem Paper	½d. and 1d.
White Tissue	1d.
Groseille	4d.
Blue	2½d.
Damask	3d.
Pomegranate	4d.

Figs. 9.6 & 9.7. Pages from *Lessons in Flower & Fruit Modelling in Wax* by the Mintorn brothers.

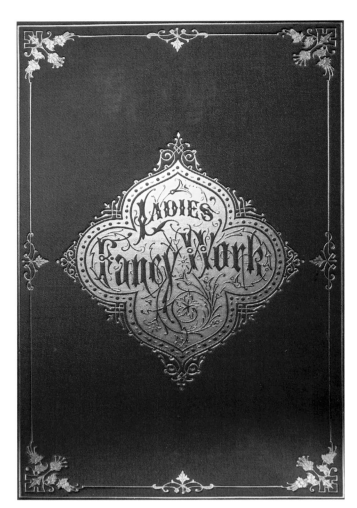

Fig. 9.8. Cover design for *Ladies Fancy Work* by Mrs. C. S. Jones & Henry T. Williams, 1877.

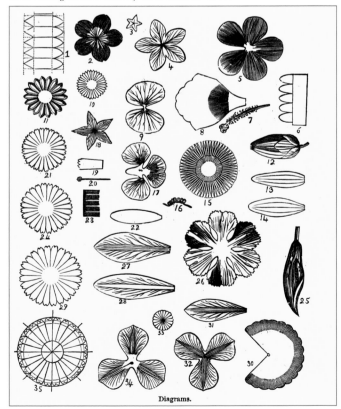

Fig. 9.9. Patterns for paper flowers from *Ladies Fancy Work.*

In *Ladies' Fancy Work, Hints and Helps to Home Taste and Recreations*, published Henry T. Williams in 1877 (Fig. 9.8), the first chapter is devoted to the art of paper flower making. Mr. Williams states, Unlike the art of forming wax-flowers, this may be made to give satisfaction in the hands of a mere tyro [novice]."

After reading a profusely illustrated thirty pages with detailed instructions, this author might choose to disagree with Mr. Williams. Patterns resembling diagrams of botanical specimens correspond to the explicit instructions to which the artist must adhere in order to create the perfect azalea, geranium, or China aster (Fig. 9.9). Illustrations such as a vase filled with tissue paper hyacinths give the reader an idea what can be accomplished (Fig. 9.10) Engravings of elegant floral sprays of morning glories and fuchsias inspire the budding paper flower artist to achieve high levels of realism (Figs. 9.11 and 9.12).

Fig. 9.10.   **Fig. 9.11.**

Fig. 9.12.

After mastering the techniques, the "flowers" of one's labors could be arranged as seen in this thirty-inch high round dome, which is bursting with blooms of many forms (Fig. 9.13). Mr. Williams would be obligated to give this presentation an A+, as he recognized the skills and virtuosity exhibited in each robust dahlia or plump camellia (Fig. 9.14). Interestingly, contrary to the popularity of paper flower making during many decades of the nineteenth century, few domed examples exist today.

Fig. 9.13. Large bouquet of paper flowers in turned wooden vase in round dome, c. 1865.

Fig. 9.14. Detail of Fig. 9.13.

Paper Houses

Not limited to flowers, paper was used to make architectural models as well. Among the Strong Museum's extensive collection this charming Gothic Revival-Style cottage was fabricated from a favorite Victorian art paper called punched paper (Fig. 9.15). This paper was sold by such companies as "Briggs & Company's Penny Packets of Superfine Perforated Cardboard for Working or Painting" (Fig. 9.16). In most cases this paper was used to create framed mottos expressing Christian values such as, "The Lord is My Shepherd," or sentimental phrases that read "Remember Me," or the popular "Home Sweet Home." With brightly colored wool or thread spelling out the message ,these could be purchased as pre-printed designs and were referred to as "perforated card work" in many of the ladies periodicals. The artist, in the case of this domed dwelling, took the medium to a different level, creating every detail from the roof cresting and bargeboard down to the picket fence in perforated paper. A miniature paper chair sits on a green velvet lawn, which is surrounded by a sand-coated walkway.

Fig. 9.15. Model of a Gothic Revival cottage in punched (perforated) paper, c. 1880. *Photo courtesy of The Strong, Rochester, New York.*

Fig. 9.16. Perforated cardboard for creating needlework mottos and designs from Briggs & Company, c. 1880.

On a more ambitious level, this paper cathedral in its original twenty-eight-inch high dome was purchased by the author from a London auction house (Fig. 9.17). Unfortunately, no artist signature or inscription identifying the cathedral accompanied this piece. It is composed of Strathmore paper, as indicated by an embossed logo on a section on its reverse side. The architectural detailing is achieved by the use of miniature embossed paper borders. The leaded glass windows are ingeniously suggested by using fine netting (Fig. 9.18). Upon inspection after its arrival from "crossing the pond," it was discovered that one spire had become detached and several of its parts (details) were missing. So, using new Bristol board, the author began to restore it to its glory by replicating those pieces. To match the effects of the aging (discoloration) of the original white paper, a pale solution of brewed tea was applied to the modern paper. One of the four lamp posts was missing, so a matching one was created using the tinted paper and a tiny blown glass ball (minus its wax coating) that was "borrowed" from a wax fruit arrangement (Fig. 9.19). The paper cathedral remains one of the finest examples created in this medium.

Fig. 9.17. A paper model of a Gothic cathedral, English, c. 1860.

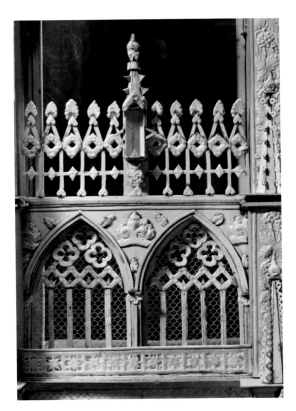

Fig. 9.18. Detail of Fig. 9.17.

Fig. 9.19.
Detail of Fig. 9.17.

Artificial Flowers in Muslin

The flowers which grace their native beds,
Awhile put forth their blushing heads;
But, ere the close of parting day,
They wither, shrink, and die away;
But these which mimic art hath made,
Nor scorched by sun nor killed by shade,
Shall blush with less inconstant hue,
Which art at pleasure can renew.

Artificial flower-making, though so elegant and ornamental an enjoyment, is one which has been, as yet, but little followed by the fair ladies of the United States, although in la belle France it has long been a favorite occupation, as much admired for its elegance as for its variety. What can be more interesting than imitating the beautiful blossoms that spring around us?

Ladies Work Department
Godey's Lady's Book
May 1847

Suggested materials were: "white and colored cambrics (muslin), prepared thread stiffened and dyed, green gauze, green raw silk, very fine yellow mohair, wires of different thicknesses, green and brown tissue paper, cotton wool, green cotton, gum water, flour, semolina, dyeing balls or saucers, vermilion, carmine, ultra-marine and indigo in powder." The tools required are similar to those for making paper flowers, with the exception of a lead weight to hold the reels of silk, a selection of goffering (cupping) tools "from the dimensions of the head of a pin to that of a small apple, a veining tool, (Fig. 9.20) a large cushion stuffed with bran, and a frame for stretching the muslin." The muslin, which is woven cotton, was to be of the finest quality. The cloth was starched and stretched on the frame for drying. Once all the materials were assembled, the process of cutting out the flower parts could commence, with *Godey's* providing illustrations depicting the petals and calyx of a simple wild rose (Fig. 9.21).

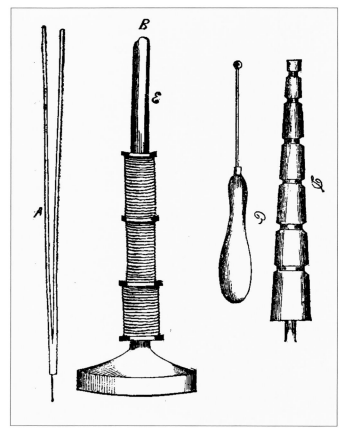

Fig. 9.20. Tools for making muslin flowers, *Godey's Lady's Book*, 1847. *Photo courtesy of the Print and Picture Collection, Free Library of Philadelphia.*

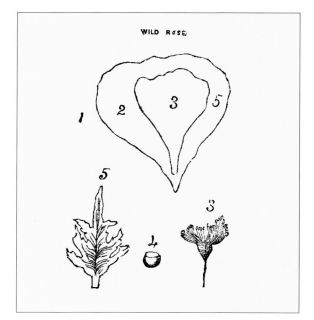

Fig. 9.21. Pattern for the Wild Rose (in muslin), *Godey's Lady's Book*, 1847. *Photo courtesy of the Print and Picture Collection, Free Library of Philadelphia.*

As pointed out by *Godey's*, the French were well advanced in the art of making artificial/muslin flowers. Pre-made arrangements of muslin flowers in vases under glass shades were available from the Silber & Fleming catalog, which sold fancy goods manufactured in Great Britain and on the continent (Fig. 9.22). This would support the concept of a cottage industry in France that could produce domed artificial flowers such as the one illustrated here (Fig. 9.23). This archetypical form consists of dyed and hand-painted muslin flowers (Fig. 9.24) that fill the oval dome, with accents of blown glass peaches and grapes. The vase is Old Paris porcelain and, as with most of these examples, has a threaded bolt underneath that secures it to the wooden base. (This proved to a practical solution for keeping the contents intact).

No. 3694 Artificial Flowers, Berries, &c., of Silk or Muslin, in Vase, with medallion portrait, under oval glass shade, fitted on gilt wooden stand; extreme height about 21 inches, length about 13 inches, width about 7¼ inches

Fig. 9.22. Muslin flowers under glass shade, Silber & Fleming Catalog, 1880. *Photo courtesy of © Victoria and Albert Museum, London.*

Fig. 9.23. Bouquet of muslin flowers with blown glass peaches and grapes in Old Paris vase, c. 1880.

Fig. 9.24. detail of Fig. 9.23.

Undoubtedly French, this twenty-eight-inch high dome of muslin flowers (one of a pair) represents the elegant style of the Second Empire of Napoleon III (Fig. 9.25 and 9.26). The gilded vase is accented with three dimensional porcelain flowers and sits on a rosewood veneered base with exquisite satinwood marquetry (Fig. 9.27). The French often used this style of base for many of their domed objects, including clocks. The flowers are beautifully rendered, with some having their edges trimmed in bright cobalt blue (Fig. 9.28).

Fig. 9.26. Detail of Fig. 9.25.

Fig. 9.27. Detail of Fig. 9.25.

Fig. 9.25. Exquisite bouquet of muslin flowers in Old Paris vase in round dome with marquetry base (one of a pair), c. 1880.

Fig. 9.28. Detail of Fig. 9.25.

The Lerman/Foy collection boasts a fine large oval dome that houses a basket of muslin flowers (Fig. 9.29). This unusual arrangement in the round is a delightful mix of silk, velvet, and gilt papers, which were used to create the central basket and the small dais that surround it. Topping these small ornate platforms are miniature gilt porcelain and wicker baskets containing glass peaches and berries (Fig. 9.30). A selection of wax melons and other fruit fills the spaces between the petite presentations. As the French would say, "C'ést magnifique!"

Fig. 9.30. Detail of Fig. 9.29.

Fig. 9.29. An elegant arrangement of muslin flowers in gilt and painted paper basket surrounded by wax and blown glass fruit in gilt miniature baskets in situ, c. 1885. *From the Leo Lerman/Gray Foy Collection.*

Fig. 9.31. A charming dome known as "The Secret Garden" depicts an idyllic scene with glass deer, birds, a pond, and a miniature Parian statue, c. 1875.

America received a taste of French floral handiwork at the Centennial Exhibition in 1876, when they viewed this showcase created by the Parisian firm of Gosse-Perier (Fig. 9.1). Jardinères mounted with porcelain plaques and bronze trim hold bouquets of artificial wild flowers, hydrangeas, and ferns. The back wall is covered in cloth ivy vines and hanging from the top is a planter filled with a striped peperomia plant created in painted silk. American businesses such as the Buffalo Decorating Co. of Buffalo, New York, exhibited artificial ivy and autumn leaves in their display at the Centennial providing a domestic resource for such items. With the commercial manufacturing of muslin flowers and foliage, the lady of the house no longer had to make her own; she could simply buy them.

A dome that is homespun in appearance and creates what this author calls "The Secret Garden" under glass, was purchased from an antique shop on Charles Street in Boston (Fig. 9.31). This idyllic setting includes a bisque statue of a child with her hands folded in prayer as she gazes heavenward (Fig. 9.32). Emerging from the muslin flowers and chenille trees are blown glass deer. Small glass birds float on the mirror pond at the base of the statue as a glass peacock takes in the view from a branch above. The artists at Disney studios could not have contrived a more charming scene.

Fig. 9.32. Detail of Fig. 9.31.

Fig. 9.33. A grouping of 19th century bead work items including (l-r) a cockatoo in gilt frame, a tea cosy, a pillow, and a bell pull, all c. 1860-1900.

To Bead or Not To Bead

Prior to World War I there was a thriving industry in the manufacturing of glass beads centered in Eastern Europe. Bohemia, once part of the Austro-Hungarian Empire, produced glass beads of the most artistic quality. Seed beads is a generic name for small beads that are classified by the aught system, size 1 (6.5 mm) being the largest to size 24 (.091 mm) the smallest. They are generally spheroidal in shape but may be tubular and are called bugle beads. Most modern beadwork uses beads in sizes 8 to15. Glass beads smaller than size 15 have not been produced since the 1890s and are referred to as "antique." It is these tiny beads that constitute the majority of the decorative beadwork of the nineteenth century. Produced in every color imaginable, they covered household items such as tea cosies, pillows, bell pulls, and framed pictures (Figs. 9.33 to 9.36). Micro-beads were the choice for creating incredibly detailed scenes, as seen on this rare beaded purse (Fig. 9.37). The subtlety of gradient values in the beads' colors gave three-dimensional qualities to each fold and shadow in this eighteenth century scene depicted entirely in glass beads. Throughout the nineteenth century ladies manuals and periodicals printed suggestions for objects that could be created or embellished by beadwork. Pre-printed designs on canvas similar to Berlin work could be purchased at needlework stores. An unadorned surface was an anathema in the Victorian interior.

Fig. 9.34 to 9.36.
Details of Fig. 9.33.

Fig. 9.37. An exceptional micro-bead work purse depicting an eighteenth century scene done entirely in glass beads, c. late 19th century. *From the Steven and Susan Goodman Collection.*

Beadwork flowers populated the interiors of many glass shades. This tall and narrow pair of domes contains arrangements of multi-colored beaded flowers (Fig. 9.38). Among the glass beads are those made of faceted metal that are referred to as "steel cuts" (Fig. 9.39). Perched atop the bouquets are doves made of muslin, along with glass grapes and cherries that provide a colorful accent. Their folky quality could identify them as American, although the use of the Old Paris vases could indicate a French origin.

Fig. 9.39. Detail of Fig. 9.38.

Fig. 9.38. A pair of narrow round domes containing bouquets of bead work flowers and blown glass fruit accents, each having a muslin covered dove at the top, all in porcelain vases, c. 1880.

Fig. 9.40. Small square-based dome with a basket of flowers done in bead work, c. 1870.

Using the suggested technique of stringing the glass beads on fine wire, this small square-based dome holds a homemade beaded basket with its glass bead flowers held in place by a mound of dried moss (Figs. 9.40 and 9.41). A delicate garland of beadwork flowers trims the top of the basket. As was the case with most parlor arts, deep oval shadowboxes provided an ideal space to display a wreath of bead work flowers (Fig. 9.42).

Fig. 9.41. Detail of Fig. 9.40.

Fig. 9.42. A walnut oval shadow box with a wreath of bead work flowers, c. 1875. *From the Steven and Susan Goodman Collection.*

Fig. 9.44.
Detail of Fig. 9.43.

Fig. 9.43. A small wicker basket of silk-on-wire flowers, c. 1880.

Smooth as Silk

Silk is thought of as one of the most luxurious of materials. Produced from the cocoons of the silkworm, the silk thread has a natural sheen that surpasses most fibers. Cloth made from silk was reserved for fabrics and clothing that could only be afforded by the wealthy. Silk embroidered garments were worn by the affluent as well as royalty. Festoons of floral designs covered the gowns of eighteenth century fashionable women, along with the waistcoats of their male counterparts.

In the Victorian era, the manufacture of fine-gauged coiled wire (as mentioned in the hair and wool work chapters) allowed ladies, in their leisure time, to create silk flowers that were more sculptural in form. The same technique used for wool flowers was employed, creating each petal of the flower in the coiled wire and then stretching the colored silk thread back and forth until the void was filled. Petals could be rounded or pointed, and be five in number to create a pansy or two dozen to create a rose. The variety of flowers was limited only by the imagination and creativity of the artist herself. The suggested form for arranging them could be in a vase or the ubiquitous basket, as seen in this example (Fig. 9.43 and 9.44). Purchased on eBay® from a home in New Jersey, this composition of silken flowers is complete with store-bought muslin leaves. Pieces of wool are used to simulate the stamens of a lily.

Fig. 9.45. A small dome of silk-on-wire flowers from the Clara Barton estate in Massachusetts, late 19th century.

What it lacks in size. this small dome more than compensates for in its provenance (Fig. 9.45). Once owned by Clara Barton, founder of the American Red Cross, it is quite simple in its design. The silk flowers and velvet leaves are wired onto a dowel rod that is glued into a drilled hole in the dome's base (Fig. 9.46). After many years of researching parlor pastimes, this author has found very little information about making silk on wire flowers.

Fig. 9.46.
Detail of Fig. 9.45.

The Seedy Side of Parlor Arts

For the first century of its existence, America was an agrarian nation. Every home that included a parcel of land had a garden for growing both ornamental plants and vegetables. A "truck patch" is an antiquated term for a backyard garden where a variety of food stuffs were grown. These sustained the owners during the warm months and, after being canned, were eaten during the cold months. Seeds were the integral part of this activity, and why shouldn't a surplus of seeds be used to fulfill a particularly artistic bent? Seed work pictures were produced predominantly during the last quarter of the nineteenth century in America. Found in deep shadowboxes, wreaths of seed work flowers gave a homey touch to the Victorian parlor. This example in a walnut and gilt frame illustrates the breadth of the seed work artist (Fig. 9.47). A proud peacock done in seeds and feathers presides over the blooms sprouting beneath him (Fig. 9.48). Many varieties of seeds encrust each petal of the various flowers, including poppy seeds, sunflower seeds, black-eyed peas, grains of wheat, and kernels of corn. One of the techniques used was to cut the petals from thin cardboard onto which seeds were glued one by one to create a lily. The other technique was that of taking a roundel of cardboard through which a wire was run

Fig. 9.48. Detail of Fig. 9.47.

Fig. 9.47. A walnut and gilt oval shadow box displaying a large wreath of seed work flowers with a seed work peacock centerpiece, c. 1875.

Fig. 9.49. A marvelous wreath of seed work flowers with hovering seed work hummingbirds in a deep gilt framed shadow box, c. 1880. *From the Steven and Susan Goodman Collection.*

Fig. 9.50. Detail of Fig. 9.49.

Fig. 9.51. Detail of Fig. 9.49.

and topping it with a mound of soft beeswax. The seeds were then imbedded into the wax to form a compound flower, such as a dahlia. These methods were also used for shell work flowers, as discussed in chapter two. Being more monochromatic in its palette, a seed work wreath in a glass sided shadow box includes some rarely seen inhabitants, seed work hummingbirds (Fig. 9.49 and 9.50). The tiny birds are poised over the large seed covered blooms with hopes of extracting some of their nectar. An unexpected addition of peanuts adds charm to this fanciful arrangement (Fig. 9.51).

The next seed work wreath example, presented in an ornately gilded oval shadowbox, would have had a much deserved place in an elegant drawing room (Fig. 9.52). Some long forgotten amateur artist must have felt much pride when this thirty by twenty-eight inch framed wreath was hung on the wall for all to admire. The flowers are composed of the similar selection of seeds as mentioned before with the addition of white rice for the huge lily, varnished walnuts as accents, and unusual flowers made from popped corn. The diversity and creativity used in pieces such as these should elevate them to a level at which they may be referred to as American folk art.

Fig. 9.52. An elegant wreath of seed work flowers in a deep ornate gilt oval frame, c. 1880. *Photo courtesy of David Klutho.*

10

AUTOMATA
"MUSICAL MECHANICAL MASTERPIECES"

Fig. 10.1. Page of "Mechanical Pieces" from the Silber & Fleming Catalog, 1880, London.
Photo courtesy of © The Victoria and Albert Museum, London.

For thousands of years man has wondered whether magic actually exists. To those who know the world of automata, magic is a certainty. The concept of making the inanimate animated is what creates the fascination with these mechanical marvels. They require the combined skills of the clockmaker, toy maker, and the costume and stage designer, and then all is set to music. In our modern day life of push button and touch screen technology, we have lost touch with that which moves by pure mechanical means. We stand in amazement before a group of colorful birds hopping from branch to branch and warbling a lovely trill, while a music box housed in an ornate base plays four different tunes, all protected under a huge glass shade (Figs. 10.2 to 10.4). We are ten years old once again.

This singing bird automaton was created by Blaise Bontems in Paris during the second half of the nineteenth century. One like it was first displayed at the Crystal Palace exhibit in 1851 with a price tag of £12 sterling, which was an extraordinary price at the time for a "toy." As an apprentice to a clockmaker in Vosages, France, along with an interest in taxidermy, Bontems set upon a long career as a maker of singing birds. He perfected the technology of simulating singing birds by studying their songs during his childhood. By using a combination of whistles and bellows he replicated the tiny chirps of hummingbirds as well as the melodic tones of warblers.

The history of musical animated devices had its origins well before Bontems set his brightly colored birds into motion. Records of automated novelties may be found in ancient times up to the Renaissance period in Europe. The eighteenth century saw such masters as Jacques de Vaucanson (1707-1782), a Frenchman who created a gilded copper duck that ate, drank, and splashed about in the water and then digested its food, presumably with the aid of chemicals (King, p. 16). A Swiss clockmaker, Pierre Jaquet-Droz (1721-1790) and Jean Frederic Leschot collaborated to create "The Writer" in 1773, which consisted of a boy draughtsman seated at a table. The highly intricate and complex mechanism within the boy's body allowed him to write sentences containing up to forty letters. These creators of such mechanical marvels toured through Europe with their "fantaisies mécanique," delighting crowds and impressing royalty.

The goal of this chapter is not to illustrate the history of automata. Several books listed in the bibliography contain more comprehensive information on the subject. The focus here is those automatons that were placed under glass and the period during which that was most prevalent, the Golden Age of Automata. Between 1850 and the First World War, Paris was the center of international fashion, where luxury items were in much demand. It provided a perfect setting for the manufacture of beautiful and highly refined automata (King, p. 22). The Marais district contained streets with rows of shops whose windows were filled with automated toys of every description. Names such as Lambert, Vichy, Roullet & Descamps, and Phalibois became synonymous with the highest quality of mechanical novelties many of which were protected under glass domes.

No. 7583.—Mechanical Bird Tree, with 15-day striking clock. Under glass shade, on black polished wood stand. Height, 28½ inches; length, 23 inches.

Fig. 10.2. Illustration of automated singing bird dome from Silber & Fleming Catalog, London, 1880. *Photo courtesy of © The Victoria and Albert Museum, London.*

Fig. 10.3. Automated singing bird dome with gilt Rococo base by Blaise Bontems, c. 1855, on an English Modern Gothic sideboard with accompanying Old Paris vases.

Fig. 10.4.
Detail of Fig. 10.3.

Scenes of Domestic Bliss and Everyday Life

As was popular in the fine arts of the nineteenth century, scenes of everyday life found their place under glass shades. A commonplace subject such as a lady reading a book (Fig. 10.5) or playing the piano (Fig. 10.6) possessed a certain element of charm that appealed to affluent buyers. These porcelain ladies of leisure were created with delicately painted bisque heads and hands, perhaps by Jumeau, a leading doll manufacturer of the time. Their bodies, which house a series of rods and gears, were carton or papier-mâché. Silk fabrics and trim were used to make the dresses designed in the latest style of the era. A well-appointed interior was suggested in this example from 1876 by Phalibois (Fig. 10.7). We find a woman seated at a sewing machine which, being a modern invention for that period, would have intrigued toy makers. This piece is marked, "EXPOSITION 1876/ J. PHALIBOIS/PARIS," which may suggest it was exhibited at the Philadelphia Centennial Exhibition of that same year.

Fig. 10.5. "Lady in the Garden" by Jean Phalibois, c. 1875. *Photo courtesy of Theriault's.*

Fig. 10.6. "Lady Seated at the Piano" by Jean Phalibois, c. 1870. *Photo courtesy of Theriault's.*

Fig. 10.7. "The Seamstress" by J. Phalibois, c. 1876. *Photo courtesy of The Murtogh D. Guiness Collection of Mechanical Musical Instruments and Automata, Morris Museum, Morristown, New Jersey, Ed Watkins Photography.*

An American trade card advertising The New Home Sewing Machine Co. of Orange, Massachusetts shows a well-dressed lady of the house peering into a looking glass that is inscribed, "Coming Events cast their Shadows before" with the image of a sewing machine beneath it (Fig. 10.8). It is unlikely a similar image would appear in a present day scenario.

Another quaint scene is depicted with this Marie Antoinette look-alike, dressed in her finest gown, whiling away some hours at her spinning wheel as an iridescent bird chirps and flutters its wings nearby on an ornate stand (Fig. 10.9 and 10.10). Having a clock in its ebonized base would make this a slightly more expensive item. Typically these domed automatons played two tunes or airs that were engaged by a pull string. The movements of the figures were generally key-wound, with a knobbed rod being pulled at the base that initiated the action. The Silber & Fleming Co. of London and Paris offered many of these "mechanically-moving figures" in their catalog of 1880 (Fig. 10.1). They provided fancy goods of all kinds to those who could afford them.

Fig. 10.8. Trade card for The New Home Sewing Machine Co., Orange, Massachusetts, c. 1875.

Fig. 10.9. "Lady at the Spinning Wheel with French Clock," c.1865. The skills of the clockmaker, automaton maker, music box maker and miniaturist are combined in this exquisite toy. *Photo courtesy of Theriault's.*

Fig. 10.10. Detail of Fig. 10.9.

Fig. 10.11. "The Organ Grinder and the Dancer" by Jean Phalibois, c. 1871. *Photo courtesy of Theriault's.*

In the nineteenth century, a familiar character on the city streets was the organ grinder. In this dome the grizzled musician, whose eyes blink and head moves side to side, turns the crank of the organ, while a pretty, porcelain-faced Gypsy girl dances to the music (Fig. 10.11). She is wearing an ethnic costume of satin and lace as she taps her tambourine (Fig. 10.12). This "scène mécanique" was created by Phalibois in the 1870s.

Another slice of life presented on a tall square base is the musical animated scene referred to as, "Stone Masons Building the Cathedral." It is an early nineteenth century piece dating to 1825 (Fig. 10.13). The Gothic-inspired cathedral is constructed of heavy cardboard and is richly ornamented with gilt arches and spires. It has five movements that involve the stone-cutters in the foreground furiously working at their crafts, chiseling, sawing, carving, and finishing. The building is set inside a papier-mâché shell that simulates the sky and a forest.

Fig. 10.12. detail of Fig. 10.11.

Fig 10.13. "Stone Masons Building the Cathedral," maker unknown, c. 1825. The clock bears the mark of "L. Marti & Cie." This piece is outstanding for its superb artistry and realistic animation. *Photo courtesy of Theriault's.*

Animated harbor scenes were depicted under glass either in deep elaborate shadow boxes, such as this one attributed to Thârin, a well-known Paris clockmaker (Fig. 10.14), or in domes as illustrated in the Silber & Fleming catalog (Fig. 10.15). In each case, the small ship bobs to and fro on a sea made of painted tissue paper while the windmill turns. In some of the upgraded models, a trestle would be in the background with a small paper train that crosses it (Fig. 10.16 and 10.17). For the most part, these scenes have pull string movements and play two tunes.

Fig. 10.14. French animated musical tableau attributed to Tharin, Paris, c. 1865. *Photo courtesy of Theriault's.*

Fig. 10.15. Illustration from the Silber & Fleming Catalog, London, 1880, "Mechanical Piece, under glass shade, representing a Landscape, with Flour Mill; one Ship sailing, etc." *Photo courtesy of © The Victoria and Albert Museum, London.*

No. 7508.—Mechanical Piece, under glass shade, representing a Landscape, with Flour Mill; one Ship sailing, which moves up and down on the imitation water; the mill-wheel revolves, the figure at foot turns the hand-wheel and causes the flour bags to ascend the lift and go into the room at the top of the house; a miller with a bag on his back comes out of the door on the left and walks to the other door, which opens at his approach and closes after him. Two airs of music. Height, 26 inches; length, 24 inches.

Fig. 10.17. Detail of Fig. 10.16.

Fig. 10.16. French animated and musical harbor scene under a glass shade with ship, flour mill, wind mill, miniature train, and clock. The backdrop is a hand-painted papier-mâché shell, c. 1880.

As cities and towns grew throughout the nineteenth century, part of their planning was the creation of parks where one could find escape from the brick and stone and the heat it generated. To sit under a huge shade tree or on a manicured lawn gave city dwellers a much desired respite. And what better to provide entertainment in this setting but a bandstand, where classical as well as popular music could be played in the cool of the evening? This form of amusement was brought into the parlor in this extraordinary, one-of-a-kind musical roundabout (Fig. 10.18) that was offered by M.S. Rau Antiques in

Fig. 10.19. Detail of Fig. 10.18.

Fig. 10.20. Detail of Fig. 10.18.

Fig. 10.18. A patriotic ivory musical roundabout featuring an all-ivory carved gazebo filled with tiny ivory orchestral members. The musical movement plays six tunes including "The Star Spangled Banner" and "The Washington Post March." The titles of each song are engraved on the miniature ivory music stands. C. 1900. *Photo courtesy of M.S. Rau Antiques, New Orleans.*

New Orleans. Every detail of the bandstand, from the conductor, the band members, and the music stands with their inscribed sheet music to the gazebo itself is made of carved ivory (Fig. 10.19 and 10.20). With a circa date of 1900, it plays six patriotic tunes, including Francis Scott Key's *The Star Spangled Banner* and John Phillip Sousa's *The Washington Post March,* as the whole interior revolves like a carousel under the glass dome. Most likely of German or French origin and made for the American market, one need only look at this confection in ivory as it spins and plays its lilting melodies and the cares of the world are momentarily forgotten.

In provincial France during the late nineteenth century and early twentieth centuries, it was customary for a bride and groom to be gifted a *globe de mariée* (trans. marriage dome) which served as a remembrance of their wedding day (Figs. 10.21 and 10.25). The bride would place her headdress, usually made of wax orange blossoms, and other mementos upon a red tufted velvet cushion surrounded by etched mirrors and ornate gilt metal decorations (Figs. 10.22 to 10.24). These marriage domes were commercially produced in the thousands and many still exist. But very few created were also music boxes, as seen in these two examples. In several cases, just as with the automated domes mentioned before, they played two airs indicated on a label pasted under the base (Fig. 10.26). The two tunes here are: "Noces de Jeanette" (Wedding of Jeanette) and "Loin du Pays" (Faraway Country). A pull-string or key wind would activate the music.

Fig. 10.21. French musical *globe de mariée* (marriage dome), c. 1901. Resting upon the velvet cushion is the bride's coronet of wax orange blossoms. Etched glass mirrors and gilt brass decorations symbolize a happy and fruitful marriage. *Photo courtesy of Theriault's.*

Figs. 10.22 to 10.24. Details of Fig. 10.21.

Fig. 10.26. Detail of label from Fig. 10.25.

2 AIRS

Noces de Jeannette
Loin du pays

Fig. 10.25. French musical *globe de mariée*, c. 1890. This example also includes the bride's wax orange blossom coronet, veil and ribbons. The label beneath the base lists the two tunes that can be played by key wind. *Photo courtesy of Theriault's.*

Monkey Business

The Great Age of Exploration of the fifteenth and sixteenth centuries brought untold treasures to European ports including porcelain, silk, and spices from the East. From South America and Africa, along with gold and silver, there came an array of exotic creatures, such as brilliantly colored parrots and monkeys. Monkeys, with their human-like expressions and amusing antics, became a favorite source of entertainment for royalty and the aristocracy. Dressed in ruffled collars and tiny silk coats, they delighted those privileged enough to be at court and soon found themselves included in paintings of the era. The term *singerie* derives from the French word for monkey, *singe,* and translates to "monkey trick." These *singerie* themes were popular throughout Europe from the Renaissance onward. It was only logical that monkeys assumed anthropomorphic roles in the decorative arts as well. During the middle of the eighteenth century the Meissen ceramic works of Germany created full monkey orchestras in porcelain (Fig. 10.27). This continued throughout the nineteenth century, and Jean Phalibois must have had this concept in mind

Fig. 10.27. Twenty-two-piece Meissen porcelain monkey orchestra, c. 19ᵗʰ century. *Photo courtesy of Christie's, New York.*

when he created this automaton of a monkey string trio (Fig. 10.28). Outfitted in their finest silk clothing, they each play their instrument while turning their papier-mâché heads and moving their leather mouths, as if singing to the music (Fig. 10.29).

The Phalibois firm became well-known for their "scènes animées" under glass shades. Jean-Marie Phalibois was born in Paris in 1835. He is first registered as a cardboard manufacturer in the Rue de Temple. In 1871, he set up shop making mechanical pictures and musical novelties in Rue Charlot. Phalibois exhibited at the Paris Universal Exhibition of 1878, showing mechanical scenes under glass domes. In 1893, Jean Phalibois retired and his son Henri took over running the firm (Robertson, p. 44).

Fig. 10.28. French musical and animated monkey string trio with harpist, violinist and cellist by Jean Phalibois, c. 1880. Each monkey turns their head and moves their lips as if singing to the two airs of music. All of the monkey automatons play two tunes.

Fig 10.29.
Detail of Fig. 10.28.

Another creation of the eighteenth century was the French farce or comedy where actors took on the roles of the aristocracy, but all the while wearing monkey masks so as not to be accused of blatant mockery. This idea became one of the mainstays of Phalibois's automated toy production, and he depicted monkeys with human bodies performing many human activities, such as an artist painting a landscape en plein air while a small bird jumps from branch to branch in the tree above (Figs. 10.30 to 10.32). This piece sold for £5 10s in 1880.

Fig. 10.30. "The Monkey Artist" by J. Phalibois, c. 1880. A well-dressed monkey is found painting a landscape en plein air with his bottle of wine close by. A clock is included in this animated scene.

No. 7591.—Mechanical Piece, under glass shade, representing a Monkey Artist painting a landscape. The figure is richly dressed in dark velvet, embroidered with gold braid. The manner in which it takes the colour from the palette and then proceeds to paint is very natural. Two airs of music. Height, 26½ inches; length, 20 inches.

Fig. 10.31. Illustration from the Silber & Fleming Catalog, London, 1880, of the Monkey Artist mechanical piece under a glass shade. *Photo courtesy of © The Victoria and Albert Museum, London.*

Fig. 10.32. Detail of Fig. 31.

Along with the artist monkey, many of these simian-themed novelties were illustrated in the Silber & Fleming catalog (Fig. 10.33). At a price of £7 10s and listed as item No. 2250, one could purchase the shooting monkey who raises his rifle and fires at the target on the opposite end of the oval dome (Figs. 10.34 and 10.35). He misses, turns his head with his mouth chattering, and raises the rifle again, fires, hits the bulls eye and up pops a bouquet of flowers.

Silber & Fleming listed item No. 2265 (Fig. 10.36) as "the Monkey Fisherman- mechanical piece, under glass shade, representing a Monkey Fisherman seated on a bank apparently smoking and fishing in a most natural manner. Two airs of music. Height 26   in.; length 20 in. £5 10s each" (Fig. 10.37).

No. 7500.—Mechanical Piece, under glass shade, representing a Monkey Figure, shooting. Two airs of music. Height, 26½ inches ; length, 20 inches.

Fig. 10.33. Illustration from the Silber & Fleming Catalog, London, 1880, representing a "Monkey Figure, shooting." *Photo courtesy of © The Victoria and Albert Museum, London.*

Fig. 10.35. Detail of Fig. 34.

Fig. 10.34. "The Marksman Monkey" by J. Phalibois, c. 1880. A monkey figure dressed in silk and lace raises his rifle to shoot at a target that eventually pops up as a bouquet of flowers.

Fig. 10.36. Illustration from Silber & Fleming Catalog, London, 1880, of a "Monkey Fisherman." *Photo courtesy of © The Victoria and Albert Museum, London.*

No. 7596.—Mechanical Piece, under glass shade, representing a Monkey Fisherman, seated on a bank, apparently smoking and fishing in a most natural manner. Two airs of music. Height, 26½ inches; length, 20 inches.

Fig. 10.37. "The Fisherman Monkey" by J. Phalibois, c.1880. As the monkey raises his pipe to his mouth and lowers his fishing rod, a small fish darts in and out from beneath the tree. *Photo courtesy of Theriault's.*

Fig. 10.38. "The Monkey Magician" by Phalibois, c. 1880, dressed in an ornate Conjuror's costume. The monocled monkey invites the viewer to a game of chance. *Photo courtesy of Theriault's.*

No. 7584.—Mechanical Piece, under glass shade, representing a Monkey Magician. Richly dressed figure standing behind a table; in each hand is a brass cover which it constantly lifts up and down, different articles appearing upon the table each time the covers are raised. Two airs of music. Height, 27½ inches; length, 20 inches.

Fig. 10.40. Illustration from Silber & Fleming Catalog, London, 1880, "The Monkey Magician." *Photo courtesy of © The Victoria and Albert Museum, London.*

A game of chance is the theme of the piece entitled, "The Monkey Conjurer," where the monkey is costumed as a mystical sorcerer dressed in elaborate silks and velvets with gold ormolu paper edging and a conical shaped hat (Figs. 10.38 and 10.39). He sports a monocle on his right eye. Standing behind a draped table he holds two silver cups that, when lifted in sequence or simultaneously, reveal five possible objects: green, orange, or white balls, die, or nothing. The monkey turns his head and nods and moves his mouth as if enticing the viewer to place a wager (Fig. 10.40). The original music label on the base lists two airs with English names, "Sweet By and By" and "Mabel Waltz," indicating its production for the English or American market. Theriault's, which is the premier name in antique doll and automata auctions, placed an estimate of US$12,000-15,000 on the Monkey Conjurer for their sale in 2005. In 1880, Silber & Fleming priced this piece at £5 5s.

Fig. 10.39. Detail of Fig. 10.38.

A rare monkey dome not featured in the catalog is "A Trip to the Dentist" (Fig. 10.41). In this somewhat macabre scene, the monkey gentleman is seated and lifts a goblet of wine to his mouth with the hope of numbing the pain as the leering dentist, with eyes blinking, looms over him, moving the dental tool closer and closer. As if responding to the dentist's command, the inebriated patient opens his mouth even wider for an easier access (Fig. 10.42). After traveling to James Julia's auction in rural Maine, the author was confronted with six phone bidders when this piece came on the block. It was a battle to the end but, with heart palpitations and beads of sweat forming, the author prevailed.

Fig. 10.42.
Detail of Fig. 10.41.

Fig. 10.43. Detail of gilt embossed paper that trims most of the elaborate costumes on the monkey figures.

Fig. 10.41. "The Dentist Monkey" by J. Phalibois, c. 1875. An intoxicated monkey gentleman opens his mouth wide as the leering monkey dentist brings the dental tool closer and closer.

Having spent thirty years teaching in public school, this author is partial to the model "The Monkey Professor and Student" (Fig. 10.44). The bespectacled professor waves his stick and moves his head and mouth as if reading from his lesson book (Fig. 10.45). The attentive student raises his right hand to write the dictated figures on the blackboard, while looking alternately at the professor then back to the board , his jaw jabbering as if in an animated exchange. No detail was spared to create this humorous scene. Within the base the governor is double-stamped "J. Phalibois Á Paris," the musical movement is stamped "J. Phalibois" on the bedplate, and an ink script on the interior of the base reads, "Maitre d'école, (Headmaster) No.3." Interestingly, Phalibois favored wooden cams rather than brass to create his automations, perhaps for economic reasons. In this case, 7 cams animate the professor and 3 cams the student.

Fig. 10.45.
Detail of Fig. 10.44.

Tobacco and smoking have had a long and checkered history dating to the first century A.D. During the late twentieth century, research exposed the ill-effects of smoking and we evolved into a society where smoking is looked upon in a negative light. The creation of non-smoking office and public buildings, as well as public transportation, restaurants and bars, has placed a stamp of disapproval on lighting a cigar, pipe, or cigarette. This was not the case during the nineteenth century. It is reported that the cigarette was invented in 1832 by Egyptian artillery men during the siege of Acre. Tubes of paper filled with gunpowder acted as devices to light and fire the cannons at an accelerated rate. The cannon crew who developed this innovative technique was rewarded with a pound of tobacco by the field commander. Not having a pipe at their disposal, the men rolled the tobacco in the paper tubes. With the first friction matches being introduced in 1852, by the 1860s the manufacture of cigarettes took hold, with millions being produced each year both in America and in Europe. Never ones to miss an opportunity, the Parisian toymakers capitalized on this and began selling models of what they advertised as "Smokers." The smokers took the forms of Chinamen with pipes, seated sultans with hookahs, mashers (men who force their unwelcomed attentions on women), huntsmen, marquises, and the "Mechanical Monkey Smoker" (Fig. 10.46). Although not originally sold under a dome, this incredible toy is now protected by a glass shade. The Monkey Smoker, or *Singe Fumeur,* was made by Gustav Vichy, c. 1875. He was advertised in the Silber catalog as a "figure richly dressed in satin and velvet. In his right hand he holds a meerschaum cigarette holder, which he raises to and from his mouth, and from which when a cigarette is put in, he smokes in a most perfect manner, moving it up and down to his mouth and puffing out the smoke. £5 5s" (Fig. 10.47 and 10.48).

The act of smoking was created by an ingeniously designed set of bellows concealed in the monkey's belly. The smoke was drawn in via a tube that ran down the right arm into the stomach, where it was then expelled by another bellows up a tube to the mouth, thus creating the illusion. All the while, this dandified ape turned his head and blinked his languid eyes as he raised a lorgnette to his face with a most disdainful look. This affected fellow was sold by Theriault's as part of The Private Collection of Christian Bailly in 2004.

Fig. 10.46. "The Smoking Monkey Marquis" or *Singe-Fumeur* by Gustav Vichy, c. 1875. This figure appeared in the department store catalog of *Au Louvre* in 1884 in the luxury category at 130 FRANCS.

Fig. 10.47. Detail of Fig. 10.46. The Monkey Marquis taking a puff from his cigarette.

Fig. 10.48. Detail of Fig. 10.48. A look of disdain as he peers through a raised lorgnette.

Fig. 10.50. Detail of Fig. 10.49.

Fig. 10.49. "French Rope Dancer with Two Musicians," maker unknown, c.1860. Up until the 1800s, rope dancing was a popular entertainment performed for royalty, as would be implied by the elaborate setting shown here. *Photo courtesy of Theriault's.*

A Taste for The Exotic and The Erotic

The Moulin Rouge and the Follies Bergère gave Belle Époque Paris the much deserved reputation of being an entertainment capital. Dancers such as La Goulue and Loïe Fuller were part of an evening's festivities, as well as acts by jugglers, acrobats, snake charmers, and contortionists. The circus also played a major role in entertaining multitudes of people, as it was developed from humble beginnings prior to the nineteenth century into a major industry by the likes of P.T. Barnum and his European counterparts. Once again, the toymakers of The Marais incorporated these popular themes into their creations. Tightrope walkers appear under glass domes as they perform jumps or pliés on a wire as accompanying musicians play their instruments (Figs. 10.49 and 10.50). Whether depicted in a sculpted paper theatrical setting befitting a Moroccan palace or in the country side under an artificial tree (Figs. 10.51 and 10.52), the mechanics used in the animations are similar. A painted and mirrored shell of papier-mâché provides an elaborate backdrop for "The Clown Juggler" (Fig. 10.53). Clowns became perfect themes for automata with their colorful makeup and costumes, along with their propensity for hilarious hijinks. The clown depicted here is typical of the white-faced, bald-capped French circus clown of the era. The animation consists of moving his legs back and forth as the striped balancing roll turns and pivots, appearing to move from foot to foot. He raises and lowers his head as the music plays two tunes.

Fig. 10.51. "The Tightrope Dancing Act" with musician and chiming clock, maker unknown, c. 1860. *Photo courtesy of Theriault's.*

Fig. 10.52. Detail of Fig. 51.

Fig. 10.53. "The Clown Juggler," attributed to Phalibois, c. 1880s. *Photo courtesy of Theriault's.*

A fascination with things "oriental" prevailed throughout the nineteenth century. As European wealth grew, so did travel to the Middle East. These faraway places with strange sounding names became the subject of literature, fine art, and the decorative arts. Tales of the Arabian Nights and images of exotic bazaars created a romanticized world in the minds of most Westerners. Turkish corners overflowing with cushions, beaded drapes, pierced brass lanterns, and hookahs became de rigueur in many homes.

A subject used by such French painters as Ingres and Lefèbvre was the odalisque or female slave who resided in the sultan's harem. Unlike other paintings of nude women depicting biblical or allegorical themes, these were of women whose purpose was to satisfy desire. The Victorian Era has become synonymous with strict standards of morality. There were well-established rules for everything, but particularly those rules associated with the physically sensual. Sexual behavior, images, and thoughts were to be suppressed. Intimate sensuality was construed as inappropriate and immoral. The glimpse of a woman's exposed ankle was scandalous. But the French have always taken a different view on sexuality. Why not take a painting of an odalisque, animate it, and set it to music, as seen in this example by Thârin of Paris entitled, "Là Joueuse de Lyre" (the Lyre Player, Fig. 10.54). Surrounded by an elegant gilded gesso-over-wooden frame, this pale paramour lounges on a divan with all the necessary accouterments in the foreground, including a slipper that has unknowingly come off. There is a key wind and a pull-string stop/start at the right side that, when engaged, causes her wrist and arm to move in a realistic manner, as though she is strumming the harp. This seductress, with her come hither look, must have made quite an impression in the salon that she originally graced.

Fig. 10.54. "La Joueuse de Lyre" (The Lyre Player) with clock by Thârin, Paris, c. 1860. An elegant representation of an odalisque seductively strumming her harp to play two tunes. *Photo courtesy of Theriault's.*

From Napoleon Bonaparte's occupation in the early 1800s to the opening of the Suez Canal in 1869, Egypt became a captivating source of design in the arts. The Egyptian Revival style in architecture and the decorative arts swept Europe and traveled to America as well. On both sides of the Atlantic, Egyptian motifs found their place on monumental buildings sporting lotus-topped columns and winged scarab lintels over doorways. Obelisks, whether ancient or newly-made, appeared in public squares and cemeteries. The tallest obelisk of all, the Washington Monument in America, opened its doors to the public in 1888, after forty years in construction. This attraction for things Egyptian took its hold on the entertainment world as well. "Little Egypt" (Farida Spyropoulos) made her dancing debut at the Egyptian Theater on the 1893 World's Columbian Exposition Midway in Chicago. Donning a costume fashioned after the Queen of the Nile, Little Egypt created a sensation as she shimmied and shook. Her dance was soon to be

Fig. 10.56. Illustration from the Silber & Fleming Catalog, 1880, London, representing (a) "Mechanical Sleeping Beauty in richly gilt moulded frame." *Photo courtesy of © The Victoria and Albert Museum, London.*

Fig. 10.55. "The Suicide of Cleopatra" by Phalibois, c. 1880. The ultimate in nineteenth century automated eroticism with rolling eyes, heaving breasts, and snakes biting at the doomed damsel, in an imposing frame 4 feet wide by 3 feet high. *Photo courtesy of The Murtogh D. Guiness Collection of Mechanical Musical Instruments and Automata, Morris Museum, Morristown, New Jersey, Tim Volk Photography.*

known as the "Hoochee-Coochee." Paris was feeling the same effects of "Egyptomania" and its alluring ways. The Phalibois firm introduced its model, commonly referred to as "The Suicide of Cleopatra" (Fig. 10.55) which was listed in the Silber & Fleming Catalog of 1880 as The Sleeping Beauty (Fig. 10.56). The catalog describes the piece as:

> a female figure 24 inches long lying on rich velvet sofa holding in her left hand a serpent which moves about and apparently bites her; her eyelids move and the eyes turn backward and forwards, the bosom moves up and down as with natural respiration; another serpent at her foot on the couch moves about. The figure is slightly dressed, etc.

The advertisement also states:

> the mechanism is set in motion by dropping a coin into the small brass opening in the front of the case. Two airs of music. [the price] £22 10 shillings.

Being coin-operated, one may assume the advertised model was intended for a public space such as a pub or an amusement hall. The example illustrated here, one of two known, is from the Murtogh D. Guinness Collection of Mechanical Musical Instruments and Automata that can be seen at the Morris Museum in Morristown, New Jersey. It is well worth the trip to the Morris Museum to see this extraordinary world class collection of musical mechanical marvels.

The Winding Down of Automatons

Another marvel of the nineteenth century was the use of electricity and its application to modern technology. Prior to the nineteenth century, static electricity and electromagnetism were theories that had existed throughout the civilized world for centuries. While the early nineteenth century saw rapid progress in electrical science, the late nineteenth century would see the greatest progress in electrical engineering. Through such people as Lord Kelvin, Alexander Graham Bell, George Westinghouse, and Thomas Edison, electricity was turned from a curiosity into an essential tool for modern life. Electricity had its impact on the automated toymakers as winding mechanisms were replaced by motors that ran by electric current. As tastes changed during the early twentieth century, the younger generation of established toy making firms turned to electrical automated figures that were used in storefronts and commercial displays. The quaint shops of the Marais closed one by one as the demand for automata dwindled and the Second Industrial Revolution, run by electricity, charged full speed into the twentieth century.

11
ESOTERICA

Fig 11.1. Illustration from *Ladies' Fancy Work*, 1877, suggesting the proper decoration of one's mantle and hearth for the summer months.

Glass domes served a multitude of purposes other than protecting the handiwork of the lady of the house, as indicated by the illustration of how to decorate one's fireplace from *Lady's Fancy Work* of 1877 (Fig. 11.1). Clocks displayed under domes were popular items. One may wonder how many domes were cracked or broken due to their being removed to wind the clock. Statues, particularly those made from Parian porcelain, retained their luminous white color while under the cover of a protective glass shade. Parian ware is a type of unglazed bisque porcelain that was created in England during the 1840s. It is named for the Greek island Paros known for its fine-textured white marble. Copies of classic marble statues, such as Hiram Powers's *The Greek Slave* (Fig. 11.2), could be reproduced in Parian and were affordable to those who wished to exhibit their awareness of popular art and culture. American sculptor, Hiram Powers (1805-1873), worked in the Neo-classical style. In 1843 he created *The Greek Slave* in life-size which became a central feature at The Crystal Palace Exhibition of 1851 in London. It quickly became a symbol for the abolishment of slavery in America and was found in many Union households.

Fig. 11.2. "The Greek Slave," a Parian porcelain copy (c. 1855) of Hiram Power's marble statue in a square-based dome with marquetry design.

Fig. 11.3. A pair of bisque figurines with gilt decoration under arbors of bisque flowers, c. 1880.

Ornamental bisque figurines, typically standing under arbors of bisque flowers, were produced commercially throughout the second half of the nineteenth century in both England and France (Fig. 11.3 and 11.4). Generally in pairs, depicting a boy and a girl in fancy dress, they were intended to be placed at either end of a mantle where they could glance furtively at each other through their glass shades. Religious figures, such as the crucifix (Fig. 11.5) and the Virgin Mary under a bower of muslin flowers (Fig. 11.6), had their place under glass in Christian homes.

The pair of carved ivory sculptures reflect the Anglo-Raj influence in home décor when Victoria reigned as Empress of India (Fig. 11.7). The skill required to produce such souvenirs is evident in the detailed carving of the parasol that shields the occupant from the intense sun (Fig. 11.8).

No. 3681 Parian Figure, under round glass shade, fitted on black wooden stand; extreme height about 18 inches, diameter about 6½ inches

No. 3682 Parian Figure, under round glass shade, fitted on black wooden stand; extreme height about 18 inches, diameter about 6½ inches

Fig. 11.4. Illustration from Silber & Fleming Catalog, London, 1880, representing bisque (Parian) figures under glass shades. *Photo courtesy of © The Victoria and Albert Museum, London.*

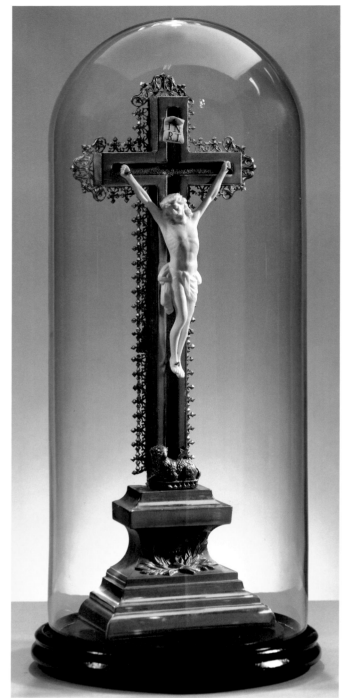

Fig. 11.5. The crucifixion of Christ, a bisque porcelain figure of Christ on a gilt bronze cross, c. 1900.

Fig. 11.6. A bisque figure of the Madonna beneath an arbor of muslin flowers, c. 1880.

Fig. 11.8.
Detail of Fig. 11.7.

Fig. 11.7. A pair of small domes containing Anglo-Raj ivory genre carvings, c. late 19th century.

For centuries itinerant women (and men) in Europe and Great Britain traveled from village to village selling everyday necessities and notions. These walking "general stores" offered everything from used toys to bolts of lace. During the Georgian and Victorian eras, dolls referred to as "pedlars" were created to mimic them. Traditionally, the dolls are depicted as old women in red hooded cloaks, similar to this one purchased from an antique shop over thirty years ago in Bath, Maine (Fig. 11.9). There must have been much excitement as these craggy-faced saleswomen entered each hamlet, offering their wares along with the news and gossip from the neighboring town. With hands and faces of leather, cloth, or papier-mâché, the pedlar doll generally carried a basket or tray filled with miniature items either found or created by the doll maker. A large pedlar doll of eighteen inches, such as the one under a mahogany-based dome, is a rare find (Fig. 11.10). She carries a bell in her right hand to announce her arrival and offers an array of tempting trinkets (Fig. 11.11 to 11.13).

Fig. 11.9. An English "pedlar" doll in glass dome, c. 1860. *From The Steven and Susan Goodman Collection.*

Fig. 11.11. Detail of Fig. 11.10.

Fig. 11.12. Detail of Fig. 11.10.

Fig. 11.10. A large 17-inch English "pedlar" doll offering an assortment of necessities and trinkets, c. 1860.

Fig. 11.13. Detail of Fig. 11.10.

A commercially produced, porcelain headed doll dressed rather elegantly in velvets and lace stands behind her booth hawking items such as crockery, a blue glass cat, and an embroidered sampler (Fig. 11.14 and 11.15). This piece from England was purchased by the author on eBay®.

Fig. 11.15. Detail of Fig. 11.14, depicting a blue glass cat with red glass eyes.

Fig. 11.14. A porcelain English "pedlar" doll in velvets and lace with her own stand where she offers her wares, c. 1860s.

The art of the confectioner is preserved under a three feet high round dome at The Strong Museum (Fig. 11.16). Made of molded sugar, this patriotic cake topper encompasses the symbols of the United States of America. Resting on an ornate base, arches supported by neoclassical caryatids surround the figure of George Washington, who is holding the Declaration of Independence in his right hand. Between the arches, three cupids proudly hold American flags aloft while the fourth cupid rings a miniature Liberty Bell that is inscribed with the date 1776. The personification of America, Columbia, holds the highest position on the very top as she waves the stars (thirteen to represent the original colonies) and stripes. There is no provenance with this piece, but one can imagine the cake that went with it. It certainly would have been worthy of any state dinner or presidential inauguration. One fancies that it, along with the cake, was part of the opening ceremonies at the Centennial Exhibition held in Philadelphia, the cradle of liberty, in 1876. Wherever it made its debut, it must have been amazing.

Another confection, in this case created in cork, is a highly-detailed steeple or clock tower from The Strong Museum (Fig. 11.17). Every architectural detail

Fig. 11.16. An extraordinary American patriotic cake topper made of molded sugar (27 inches high) commemorating the 1876 Centennial of the United States. *Photo courtesy of The Strong, Rochester, New York.*

Fig. 11.17. A highly detailed scale model of a Gothic clock tower (29 inches high) done in cork, probably English, c. late 19th century. *Photo courtesy of The Strong, Rochester, New York.*

is replicated in cork. The natural pores in the cork create the texture of weathered stone in this thirty-inch high clock tower. Cork work was another parlor pastime and the subject was usually castles or ruins. These "pictures without paint" were largely inspired by Sir Walter Scott's Waverley novels and the Romantic Revival (Howe, p. 129). Requiring simple tools and materials, such as a sharp penknife, scissors, glue, and sheets of cork, picturesque subjects could be created by the amateur and the professional cork artist. It was

suggested that ladies should include these materials when they traveled, so, if they happened upon an ivy covered ruin, they could capture it in cork.

Often entire scenes, such as this large diorama in its original Modern Gothic frame, include castles, towns, rivers, hillsides, and forests masterfully cut out of thin sheets of cork (Fig. 11.18 to 11.20). On rare occasion the name of the actual castle or setting will be inscribed on the back, but predominantly most depict romanticized visions.

Fig. 11.18. A 19th century vignette featuring a large English cork work landscape of castles, forests, boats, and villages in its original Modern Gothic frame. The cork work is flanked by a pair of carved cat plaques by Bruce Talbert, who also designed the ebonized sideboard beneath them, all c. 1860-1880.

Fig. 11.19. Detail of Fig. 11.18.

Fig. 11.20. Detail of Fig. 11.18.

Travel in the nineteenth century became more readily available with the invention of the steam locomotive in England in the early 1800s. By 1860, railways linked many of the cities and towns throughout Great Britain and Europe. On May 10, 1869, the last spike of the Transcontinental Railroad in America was driven at Promontory Summit, Utah, which eventually led to the uniting of the Atlantic and Pacific Oceans by rail. No longer did goods have to be carried by horse-drawn coaches or canal barges, or shipped by sea. It was the age of the locomotive, and with it came accessibility. A by-product of this evolution in travel was the traveling salesman. Whether selling fancy goods or farm equipment, the very latest could be brought directly to the consumer. Having more impact than pictures in a catalog, the salesman could show the potential buyer a scaled down sample of the product. These salesman samples included furniture, bathroom fixtures, or an ornate fireplace insert, as seen here under its original dome (Fig. 11.21). The lady of the house could see in three dimensions the gleaming nickel and gilt plated brass surround, grate, and fender. What a practical way to allow her to envision such an elegant addition to her front parlor or sitting room.

Fig. 11.21. A rare salesman sample of a nickel-plated and gilt bronze fireplace insert with fender, grate and fireplace tongs, c. 1860.

Scale models came in all shapes and forms. One such group is referred to as "Prisoner of War" models. The prisoners were predominantly Frenchmen who were held in British prisons during the Napoleonic Wars of 1803-1815. While in prison for years at a time, they began carving models from dried and bleached mutton and beef bones; they used the models as barter to supplement their meager rations. The typical carvings were of warships with full details of their rigging, decks, and gunnery. Some of the rarer carvings were of a popular form of execution, the guillotine (Fig. 11.22). This working bone model of a guillotine under its glass shade comes complete with its unfortunate victim, who is attired in a sailor uniform of the era. Having his hands tied and feet shackled, he is laid prone on the platform in position for the chop. With the pull of a tiny pin the blade drops and so does his head, into the pierced-carved basket (Fig. 11.23). The blade is attached to the head unit, and when it is raised the head returns to its original position and the stage is set for another macabre performance. The guillotine, with its tri-color French flag, is ornately carved and sits on a base of straw work done in a herringbone pattern. The only indication of a signature is the word *"NOM"* (French for name) and the number *"31"* etched into the base. Was this the number of people executed or the prisoner's identification?

Fig. 11.23. Detail of Fig. 11.22. The hapless victim ready for the chop.

Fig. 11.22. A prisoner of war working guillotine carved from beef or sheep bones by a French inmate during the Napoleonic Wars, c. 1803-1815, while imprisoned in Great Britain.

Fig. 11.24. An unusual tree and base done in the "Black Forest-style" under a tall oval dome, possibly late 19th-early 20th century. *From the Leo Lerman/ Gray Foy Collection.*

Another domed object from the Lerman/Foy collection proves to be an enigma to this author. The item in question is a tall narrow oval dome that covers a naturalistic carved wooden tree that grows from a highly carved base of the same wood (Fig. 11.24). At first glance one gets the impression of a Chinese influence, but upon closer examination, the carving could be that commonly known as "Black Forest." Interestingly enough, the author discovered that the term Black Forest (from Der Schwarzwald region in Germany) is a misnomer when describing such fine wood carvings. The antique carved bears, owls, chamois, and cuckoo clocks so desired by today's collectors come from the small town of Brienz, Switzerland. Regardless, what was the purpose of this tree under glass? Was it meant to hold ornaments during festive occasions or does it exist for its sculptural beauty alone?

Whether they were used to contain an artistic arrangement derived from a parlor pastime or to protect a rare artwork, such as carved wooden tree, empty domes could be purchased from a variety of sources. Multitudes of glass domes were manufactured in three basic shapes: round, square-based, and oval-based. The range in size and dimensions is mind boggling. Domes were made extensively in Great Britain, France, Germany, and to some extent in America. It is rare to find the manufacturer's label on the base of the dome such as these two from England (Fig. 11.25 and 11.26). Advertisements for empty domes were seen in the Silber & Fleming catalog and other English ads (Fig. 11.27). Taxidermists as well as clockmakers kept a ready supply on hand. An American advertisement from a business in Chicago, circa 1900, sold "Glass Shades for American and French Clocks" (Fig. 11.28). A chart of prices with a formula for determining the number of inches to be charged for a particular dome is somewhat complicated. They use as an example an oval glass shade 5 inches deep by 10 inches wide by 15 inches high.

Once the height		15
Twice the large diameter [w]	10	20
Once the small diameter [d]		5
Over [premium for oval shade]		3
	No. 43	$3.40
Oval stand, 10 inches	15¢	1.50
Box and packing		.49
	Total	$5.39

This small to medium-sized dome would have cost $5.39, the equivalent to several days' wages for the common laborer. Glass domes were not inexpensive items. The ad also specifies that any shade totaling over 80 inches would have a special price. In regards to shipping, they state, "we cannot hold ourselves responsible for breakage, hence Glass Shades are always shipped at purchaser's risk." Unfortunately, this may apply to most of today's shipping methods.

Antique glass domes may still be purchased today. In the United States, Ben Bowen of Dowling Park, Florida, offers a wide selection of antique round, oval, and square-based shades. He also sells reproduction domes. In Great Britain, they can be purchased from Antique Glass Domes, West Sussex, U.K., which carries a selection of antique domes in all shapes and sizes. As during the nineteenth century, round based domes are not as expensive as oval and square-based domes.

How does one tell if the dome is original or antique? First, if it is covering an arrangement of wax flowers or stuffed birds, how does it fit the composition? Generally the contents of the dome fit the contour of the glass very closely. Barring any warping of its wooden base, does it fit well into the routed groove? Antique domes have certain characteristics not found in modern domes. Nineteenth century glass will exhibit imperfections such as bubbles, waviness, and sometimes bits of silica that

Figs. 11.25 & 11.26. Labels found beneath the bases of English domes.

Fig. 11.27. English advertisement for glass shades, c. mid-19th century. *Photo courtesy of P. Morris.*

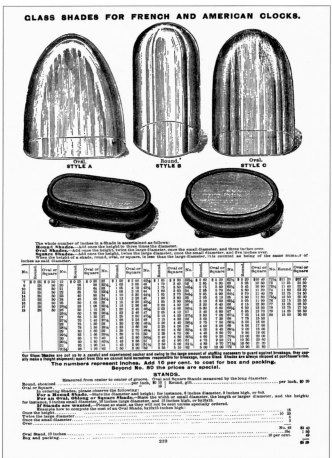

Fig. 11.28. Advertisement from a Chicago catalog selling glass shades for French and American clocks, c. 1900.

never fully liquified. The glass of an antique dome is very thin, measuring 1-2.5 millimeters depending on the size of the dome. The bottom edge of an antique dome should be rough to the touch. Most modern domes have smooth, rolled edges. Also, with many antique domes, there is a remanent of a paper strip around the bottom which may have been put there to promote a cleaner cutting of the glass.

This would be a good opportunity to discuss the difference between a dome and a bell jar. A bell jar was used primarily for scientific and horticultural purposes due to its bell shape, heavier glass, and its having a knob at the top for lifting on and off. A dome, or shade, as referred to prior to the twentieth century, was made of thin glass and used to protect various decorative items found throughout the home.

Fig. 11.29. A vignette showing an American marble mantelpiece holding a bird dome as well as a rare pair of Limoges vases (for the American market) that illustrate the story of *Uncle Tom's Cabin*, c. 1855. The leaded and enameled glass fire screen is English Aesthetic Movement in style, c. 1880.

12

GONE BUT NOT FORGOTTEN

Being an early member of the so-called "baby boomer" generation, the author had a direct link to the nineteenth century through both sets of grandparents, who were born in the 1880s. Stories of their childhoods and young adulthoods growing up in rural Pennsylvania on the paternal side and in Gratz, Austria, on the maternal side, were fascinating. Knowing people that lived in a world without electricity, telephones, automobiles, and airplanes gives one a perspective that the younger generations of today could not comprehend. It was a slower, quieter world, where people aspired to good manners. As we begin our travel into the twenty-first century, what would be the appeal for a time so long ago? Might we wish for a time when words such as sentimentality, romanticism, and charm come to mind? The high tech world of today allows us to send images and messages within seconds to anyone, anywhere in the world. We are

rapidly losing something that the Victorians held in high esteem: the ability to write a letter. E-cards have eliminated the need to go to a store and select a card for a special occasion. Our modern lives have become dependent on touch screens and keyboards. For those of us who look back upon the nineteenth century with interest and fondness, it may provide a sense of nostalgia for a time when life was simpler.

The Victorian era was also a time when people took great pride in what they created, whether it was a pair of shoes manufactured in a factory or a bouquet of wax flowers made as a parlor pastime. Things created by hand, using quality materials, were the rule, not the exception. The intention of this chapter is to illustrate the concept that this pride in workmanship still exists in artists like those featured here, who have put their own twist on art forms from the nineteenth century.

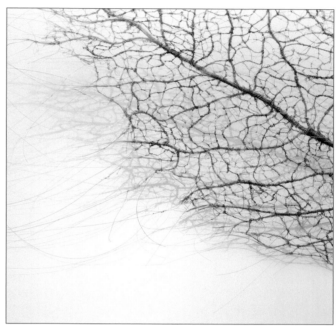

Clockwise from top left:

Fig. 12.1. Skeletonized leaf. *Photo courtesy of Michael Sage.*

Fig 12.2. Woven hair leaf (detail). *Photo courtesy of Jenine Shereos.*

Fig. 12.3. "Chrysalis" shell valentine. *Photo courtesy of Sandi Blanda.*

Fig. 12.4. "Poppies" (detail). *Photo courtesy of Justine Smith.*

Money Makes the World Go Round
Justine Smith: Paper Artist

Paper has always been a primary material in the work of Justine Smith. Her current work is the concept of money and how it touches every aspect of our lives. She is interested in the power of money and the conduit, and with the value systems with which we surround it. On a physical level a banknote is just a piece of paper, but it is what a banknote represents that is central to Smith's work. Through her collages, prints, and sculptures, she examines our relationship with money in a political, moral, and social sense, while also exploiting the physical beauty of the notes. She has created a series of botanically correct paper flowers that she displays under domes. Using acute selectivity, she composes a grouping of poppies from Chinese Yuan (Figs. 12.7 and 12.8). Choosing the currency of her homeland she creates an ethereal stand of snowdrops from English pound notes (Fig. 12.5 and 12.6). This young artist lives and works in London.

Fig. 12.5. "Snowdrops" created from English pound notes. *Photo courtesy of Justine Smith.*

Fig. 12.6. Detail of Fig. 12.5.

Fig. 12.7. "Poppies" created from Chinese Yuan. *Photo courtesy of Justine Smith.*

Fig. 12.8. Detail of Fig. 12.7.

Hair Raising Art
Jenine Shereos: (Hair) Fiber, Textile and Installation Artist

Jenine Shereos is a sculpture and installation artist who lives and works in Boston, Massachusetts. She specializes in fiber and textile processes. Jenine chose human hair as one of her mediums and has incorporated its delicate nature into a series of woven hair leaves (Fig. 12.9 to 12.12). In this series the intricacies of a leaf's veining are recreated by wrapping, stitching, and knotting together strands of human hair. She began by stitching individual strands of hair by hand onto a water-soluble backing material. At each point where one strand of hair intersects another, she stitched a tiny knot, so that when the backing was dissolved, the entire piece was able to hold its form. As Ms. Shereos states on her website, it is "the delicate trace of a hair falling silently, imperceptibly, from one's head becoming the veins of a leaf as it falls from a tree leaving its indelible imprint on the ground below." No Victorian could have put it more appropriately.

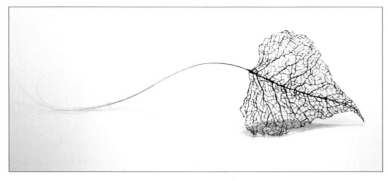

Fig. 12.9. Woven and knotted hair (work) leaf. *Photo courtesy of Jenine Shereos.*

Fig. 12.10. *Photo courtesy of Jenine Shereos.*

Fig. 12.11. *Photo courtesy of Jenine Shereos.*

Fig. 12.12. Detail of Fig. 11.

She Sells Seashells
Sandi Blanda: Shell Artist

Sandi Blanda spent most of her life growing up on Long Island, New York, admiring seashells as she walked along the beach. She was inspired to design Sailor's Valentines when she first saw one in 1983. Sandi set out to educate herself about this romantic folk art that instantly captured her heart. As a self-taught folk artist, she re-interprets antique mosaic designs with shell flowers incorporated into both single and double traditional octagonal boxes made from cherry or mahogany woods. She prefers to use unconventional messages (and titles) such as, "Go Fish" (Fig. 12.13) and "Chrysalis" (Fig. 12.14). Sandi's work has been exhibited in New York, Cape Cod, and London, and has received numerous awards. By taking a different approach, Sandi's shell work valentines represent a fresh look at an art form that was so appreciated by the nineteenth century sense of beauty and sentimentality. Sandi is represented by Quester Gallery in Rowayton, Connecticut.

Fig. 12.13. "Go Fish" shell work valentine by Sandi Blanda. *Photo courtesy of Glenn Bassett.*

Fig. 12.14. "Chrysalis" shell work valentine by Sandi Blanda. *Photo courtesy of Glenn Bassett.*

Fig. 12.15. "Snow Squall" shell work valentine by Sandi Blanda. *Photo courtesy of Glenn Bassett.*

Still Beautiful In Death
Michael Sage: Skeleton leaf Artist

Of all the parlor pastimes Victorians put under glass, the phantom bouquet is the rarest. Due to their extreme fragility, very few examples exist, and as seen from the illustrations depicted in this book, the leaves have yellowed with age and the velvet on which they are mounted has faded. Artist Michael Sage of Vancouver, Washington, is a modern day skeletonizer who has revived this art. Surrounded by an artistic family, it was only natural that Michael developed an aptitude for all things related to color, form, and texture. He was first drawn to the medium of wood and pursued a degree in the arts, with an emphasis in fine woodworking from an upstate New York college. Influenced and inspired by the likes of such studio artists as Sam Maloof, Wendel Castle, and James Krenov, he designed and produced turnings and fine boxes that sold in galleries throughout the United States.

In 1994, Michael was given a skeleton leaf by a woodturning friend. He had seen leaves desiccated by insects while exploring neighboring woods as a boy, but they did not have the same effect on him as this did. He was soon consumed by the idea of skeletonizing leaves and made it his mission to learn everything he could about the process and the art form. Gathering every historical image and literary reference, he has compiled an extensive archive on the subject. He has developed techniques for making the leaves more resistant to the ravages of time and has put his own artistic twist on their presentation (Fig. 12.16). Still utilizing the idea of the shadow box, his approach is that of a graphic, contemporary look. Ignoring the edicts of Edward Parrish and other skeletonizers of the nineteenth century, Michael incorporates eye catching color in his designs (Fig. 12.17). And pushing the envelope even further, he has created a dress entirely composed of skeleton leaves that he displays on a mannequin, whose title is simply "Eve" (Figs. 12.18 and 12.19). One could only imagine a series of these lacy foliated fashions gracing a New York or Paris runway.

Fig. 12.16. *Photo courtesy of Michael Sage.*

Fig. 12.17. *Photo courtesy of Michael Sage.*

Figs. 12.18 & 12.19. "Eve" by Michael Sage. A different twist on the little black dress. *Photos courtesy of Michael Sage.*

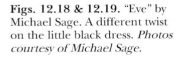

Hope Springs Eternal

Parlor pastimes are just that; they come from times in the past. The old adage of "what goes around, comes around" may or may not apply when it comes to the art of making wax flowers or hair work, but it is through artists such as those mentioned above, that art made by hand will continue to exist, at least in some small way, as long as man possesses the desire to create.

They Are Still Making Them

Another unanswered question is, how were glass domes made in the past? The tense of that question requires some modification because glass domes are still being made. To this author's knowledge, most modern domes are manufactured in Europe. One such company is ide.co Glass Studios® in Germany, which has generously donated images showing the processes of creating a glass dome.

The process of glassblowing has remained unchanged for centuries. The molten portion of glass, known as the gather, is taken from the furnace at a temperature of 2400º F (1320º C). It is attached to the preheated end of the blowpipe and is allowed to fine out (allowing bubbles to rise) at a temperature of 2000º F (1090 C). It is then rolled on the marver, a steel plate, to achieve the desired shape, and is periodically reheated in a furnace called a glory hole to keep it malleable at 1600-1900º F (871-1038º C).

The glass worker begins to blow and create the first bubble of glass, called the parison. He then stands high over the mold and blows the glass into the form. The blown form is removed from the mold and, by heating the blowpipe end, it is transferred to another rod called the punty or pontil for final shaping. Finally it is cut from the rod and placed in the lehr or annealer, the final furnace, at a temperature between 700 and 900º F (371 and 482º C). The annealing or tempering process may take several hours to several days, depending on the size of the dome, and will prevent the glass from cracking due to future thermal stress. When thoroughly cooled, the base of the dome is cut and polished. Generally, four people, including the moldmaker, are involved in the creation of a blown glass dome. ide.co Glass Studios® makes a variety of shaped domes including round, oval, and square-based. They will also do custom sizes.

Fig. 12.20. The birth of a dome. The gather of molten glass is rolled on a sheet of steel to establish the shape. *Courtesy of ide.co Glass Studios.*

Fig. 12.21. A crucible being used to reheat the gather to keep it malleable. *Courtesy of ide.co Glass Studios.*

Fig. 12.22. The first bubble or parison created by the glassblower. *Courtesy of ide.co Glass Studios.*

Fig. 12.23. The glassblower stands high above the mold and blows the glass into the given shape. *Courtesy of ide.co Glass Studios.*

Fig. 12.24. A blown glass dome nearing completion, ready to be removed from the pontil. *Courtesy of ide.co Glass Studios.*

Fig. 12.25. ide.co Glass Studios supplied domes for the "300 Years of Porcelain" exhibition at the Frankfurt Fair in 2010. *Courtesy of ide. co Glass Studios.*

"Le Salon des Fleurs"

Dating to 1829, The Philadelphia International Flower Show is the largest indoor flower show in the world. It is the main annual event of The Pennsylvania Horticultural Society (founded in 1827) with an attendance of over 250,000 people each year. In 2009, this author approached Jane Pepper, then president of the Horticultural Society, with the idea of having an exhibit that featured antique domes that contained flowers made of wax, sea shells, wool, etc. She immediately introduced the author to Sam Lemheney, who is the director of the flower show. After Sam visited the collection, he said he had the perfect fit: the 2011 flower show with Paris as its theme. He then introduced the author to Jamie Rothstein of Jamie Rothstein Distinctive Designs, who had produced extraordinary floral exhibits at the show for over twenty years. And so the seeds of "Le Salon des Fleurs" were sown. Over a period of a year and a half, an intense collaboration took place that culminated in the creation of a salon of flowers that evoked the era of Napoleon III. The exhibit included over one dozen domes from the author's collection, including a dome in progress being created by the lady of the house. "Le Salon des Fleurs" swept all the awards, five in total, including the People's Choice Award.

Fig. 12.26.

Fig. 12.27.

Fig. 12.28.

Fig. 12.29.

Fig. 12.30.

Fig. 12.31. "Le Salon des Fleurs," Philadelphia International Flower Show, 2011.

ENDNOTES

Chapter 1
1. Pepper, Charles and Madame Elise, *The Art of Making Wax Flowers & Fruit.* (London: J.Barnard & Son, 1858), pg. 7.
2. Howe, Bea, *Antiques from the Victorian Home.* (London: Spring Books, 1989), pg. 149.
3. Ibid, pg. 146.
4. Ibid, pg. 147.
5. Ibid, pg. 147.

Chapter 4
1. Frost, Christopher, *A History of British Taxidermy.* (Copyright Christopher Frost, 1987), pg. 18.
2. Browne, Montagu, *Pratical Taxidermy, A Manual to the Amateur in Collecting, Preserving, and Setting Up Natural History Specimens of All Kinds.* (London: L. Upcott Gill, 1884), pg. 16.
3. Ibid, pg. 65.
4. Ibid, pg. 63.
5. Ibid, pg. 68.

Chapter 5
1. Howe 1989, pg. 133.

Chapter 6
1. Tilton, J. E., *Phantom Flowers: A Treatise on the Art of Producing Skeleton Leaves.* (New York: Hurd & Houghton, 1864) pg. 22.
2. Parrish, Edward, *The Phantom Bouquet.* (Philadelphia: J. B. Lippincott & Co., 1863), pg. 42.
3. Ibid, pg. 39.
4. Ibid, pg. 43.

Chapter 7
1. Howe 1989, pg. 154.

Chapter 8
1. Howe 1989, pg. 194.
2. Howe 1989, pg. 194.
3. Howe 1989, pg. 198.

Chapter 10
1. King, Constance, *A Guide to Metal Toys & Automata.* (Wigston, Leicester, UK: Magna Books, 1992), pg. 22.
2. Robertson, Andrea, *Museum of Automata.* (Tower Street, York: The Museum of Automata, 1992), pg. 44.

Chapter 11
1. Howe 1989, pg. 129.

REFERENCES

Antique Glass Domes (U.K.), www.antiqueglassdomes.co.uk
Ben Bowen (USA), www.glassdomes.com
Butterfly Art Works, www.butterflyartworks.us
Ide.co Glass Studios, www.glassdomes.de
Jenine Shereos, www.jenineshereos.com

Justine Smith, www.justinesmith.net
Michael Sage, www.phantomleaves.com
Rapunzel's Delight, www.rapunzelsdelight.com
Sandi Blanda, sgblanda@aol.com
The Antique Room, Atlantic Ave. Brooklyn, New York
Theriault's, www.theriaults.com

BIBLIOGRAPHY

Atterbury, Paul. *The Parian Phenomenon, A Survey of Victorian Parian Porcelain Statuary & Busts.* Somerset, England: Richard Dennis Publishing, 1989.

Bailly, Sharon and Christian. *Oiseaux de Bonheur, Tabatieres et Automates (Flights of Fancy, Mechanical Singing Birds.* Antiquorium Editions, June 2001. Text in French and English.

Baird, Rosemary. *Goodwood, Art, Architecture, Sport and Family.* London: Francis Lincoln Limited, 2007.

Bishop, Robert, and Patricia Coblentz. *The World of Antiques, Art, and Architecture in Victorian America.* New York: E.P. Dutton, 1979.

Bridgeman, Harriet, and Elizabeth Drury. *The Encyclopedia of Victoriana.* New York: Macmillan Pub. Co., 1975.

Browne, Montagu. *Pratical Taxidermy, A Manual to the Amateur in Collecting, Preserving, and Setting Up Natural History Specimens of All Kinds.* London: L. Upcott Gill, 1884.

Everett, Michael. *The Birds of Paradise.* New York: G. P. Putnam's Sons, 1978.

Field, June. *Collecting Georgian and Victorian Crafts.* New York: Charles Scribner's Sons, 1973.

Fondas, John. *Sailors' Valentines.* New York: Rizzoli International Publications, 2002.

Francis, G. W. *The Art of Modelling Wax Flowers, Fruit, etc., etc.* London: Simpkin, Marshall & Co., 1854.

Frost, Christopher. *A History of British Taxidermy.* Copyright Christopher Frost, 1987.

Grenier-Snyder, Ellen M. *Musical Machines and Living Dolls, The Murtogh D. Guiness Collection of Mechanical Musical Instruments and Automata.* Morristown, New Jersey: Morris Museum, 2011.

Hale, Sarah. *Godey's Lady's Book.* Philadelphia: 1840-1890.

Henderson, Marjorie, and Elizabeth Wilkinson. *Whatnot: A Compendium of Victorian Crafts & Other Matters.* New York: William Morrow & Company, Inc., 1977.

Hillier, Mary. *Automata & Mechanical Toys.* London: Bloomsbury Books, 1988.

Howe, Bea. *Antiques from the Victorian Home.* London: Spring Books, 1989.

Jones, Mrs. C. S., and Henry T. Williams. *Ladies Fancy Work Hints and Helps to Home Taste and Recreations.* New York: Henry T. Williams, Publisher, 1877.

Jones, Mrs. C. S., and Henry T. Williams. *Household Elegancies, Suggestions in Household Art and Tasteful Home Decorations.* New York: Henry T. Williams, Publisher, 1877.

King, Constance. *A Guide to Metal Toys & Automata.* Wigston, Leicester, UK: Magna Books, 1992.

Krauss, Helen K. *Shell Art.* New York: Hearthside Press Inc., 1965.

Laird, Mark (ed.), and Alicia Weisberg-Roberts, (ed.). *Mrs. Delany & Her Circle.* London: Yale University Press, 2009.

Latham, Jean. *Victoriana, A Guide for Collectors.* New York: Stein & Day, 1971.

Laver, James. *Victoriana.* Princeton: The Pyne Press, 1975.

Leopold, Allison Kyle. *Victorian Splendor Recreating America's 19th Century Interiors.* New York: Stewart, Tabori and Chang, 1986.

Mauries, Patrick. *Shell Shock: Conchological Curiosities.* London: Thames and Hudson Lmtd., 1994.

Mearns, Barbara and Richard. *The Bird Collectors.* London: Academic Press, 1998.

Mintorn, J. H. *Lessons in Flower and Fruit Modelling in Wax.* London: George Rutledge & Sons, 1844.

Morris, P. A. *A History of Taxidermy: Art, Science, and Bad Taste.* Ascot: MPM Publishing, 2010.

Morris, P.A. *Edward Gerrard & Sons: a taxidermy memoir.* Ascot: MPM, 2004.

Morris, P.A., and M. Freeman. *Hutchings: The Aberystwyth Taxidermists.* Ascot: MPM, 2007.

Morris, P.A. *Rowland Ward–Taxidermist to the World.* Ascot: MPM, 2003.

Morris, P. A., and R. Chinnery. *The King's Choice: George W. Quatremain, Artist and Taxidermist.* Ascot: MPM, 2006.

Morris, P.A. *Van Ingen & Van Ingen: Artists in Taxidermy.* Ascot: MPM, 2006.

Morris, P.A. *Walter Potter and his Museum of Curious Taxidermy.* Ascot: MPM Publishing, 2008.

Norbury, James. *The World of Victoriana.* London: Hamlyn Publishing Group, 1972.

Parrish, Edward. *The Phantom Bouquet.* Philadelphia: J. B. Lippincott & Co., 1863.

Peacock, Molly. *The Paper Garden, Mrs. Delany (begins her life's work) At 72.* London: Bloomsbury Publishing, 2011.

Pepper, Charles, and Madame Elise, *The Art of Making Wax Flowers & Fruit.* London: J.Barnard & Son, 1858.

Revi, Albert Christian. *The Spinning Wheel's Complete Book of Antiques.* New York: Grosset & Dunlap, 1977.

Robertson, Andrea. *Museum of Automata.* Tower Street, York, YO1 1SA, U.K. 1992.

Ruhling, Nancy, and John Crosby Freeman. *The Illustrated Encyclopedia of Victoriana: A Comprehensive Guide to the Designs, Customs, and Inventions of the Victorian Era.* Philadelphia/London: Running Press, 1994.

Schultes, Richard Evans, and William A. Davis. *The Glass Flowers at Harvard.* The Botanical Museum at Harvard University. Cambridge, MA. First published by E.P. Dutton, New York. 1982.

Schwartz, Marvin, and Betsy Wade. *The New York Times Book of Antiques.* New York: Quadrangle Books, 1972.

Teale, Edwin Way. *Audubon's Wildlife.* New York: The Viking Press, 1964.

The Victorian Pattern Glass & China Book, The classic Victorian illustrated catalog of English and foreign ornamental tableware, glassware, and decorative household goods. A reprint of the Silber & Fleming Catalog, London, 1884, New York: Arch Cape Press, 1990.

Theriault. Florence. *Dolls in Motion: 1850-1915.* Annapolis Maryland: Gold Horse Publishing, 2000.

Theriault, Florence. *From the Golden Age of Automata: The Private Collection of Christian Bailly.* Annapolis, Maryland: Gold Horse Publishing, 2004.

Theriault, Florence. *Music, Motion, fancy; Rare Automata From The Golden Age.* Annapolis, Maryland: Gold Horse Publishing, 2008.

Theriault, Florence. *Playing Their Parts, 19th Century Automata, Musical Boxes and Singing Birds.* Annapolis, Maryland: Gold House Publishing, 2005.

Theriault, Florence., *When the Circus Came to Town.* Annapolis, Maryland: Gold Horse Publishing, 2007.

Tilton, J. E. *Phantom Flowers: A Treatise on the Art of Producing Skeleton Leaves.* New York: Hurd & Houghton, 1864.

Tilton, J. E. *Wax Flowers: How To Make Them. With New Methods of Sheeting Wax, Modelling Fruit, Etc.* Boston: S.W. Tilton & Co. 1864.

Toller, Jane. *Regency and Victorian Crafts; Or The Genteel Female–Her Arts and Pursuits.* London and Sydney: Ward Lock LTD., 1969.

Yates, Raymond F. and Marguerite W. *Early American Crafts and Hobbies: A Treasury of Skills, Avocations, Handicrafts, and Forgotten Pastimes from the Golden Age of The American Home.* New York: Wilfred Funk Inc., 1954.

INDEX